Writing Papers in Psychology

EIGHTH EDITION

Ralph L. Rosnow and Mimi Rosnow

WADSWORTH
CENGAGE Learning™

Australia • Brazil • Japan • Korea • Mexico • Singapore • Spain • United Kingdom • United States

WADSWORTH
CENGAGE Learning™

Writing Papers in Psychology,
Eighth Edition
Ralph L. Rosnow and
Mimi Rosnow

Psychology Editor:
Erik Evans

Assistant Editor: Gina Kessler

Editorial Assistant: Rebecca
Rosenberg

Technology Project Manager:
Lauren Keyes

Marketing Manager: Michelle
Williams

Marketing Assistant: Melanie
Cregger

Marketing Communications
Manager: Linda Yip

Project Manager, Editorial
Production: Katia Huang

Creative Director: Rob Hugel

Art Director: Vernon Boes

Print Buyer: Judy Inouye

Permissions Editor: Timothy Sisler

Production Service:
International Typesetting and
Composition

Copy Editor: Margaret Ritchie

Illustrator: International
Typesetting and Composition

Cover Designer: Dare Porter

Cover Image: © Masterfile
Corporation

Compositor: International
Typesetting and Composition

For product information and technology assistance, contact us at
Cengage Learning Customer & Sales Support,
1-800-354-9706
For permission to use material from this text or product, submit
all requests online at **cengage.com/permissions.**
Further permissions questions can be emailed to
permissionrequest@cengage.com.

Library of Congress Control Number: 2007939289

ISBN-13: 978-0-495-50956-1
ISBN-10: 0-495-50956-6

Wadsworth
10 Davis Drive
Belmont, CA 94002-3098
USA

Cengage Learning is a leading provider of customized learning
solutions with office locations around the globe, including
Singapore, the United Kingdom, Australia, Mexico, Brazil, and Japan.
Locate your local office at **international.cengage.com/region.**

Cengage Learning products are represented in Canada by Nelson
Education, Ltd.

For your course and learning solutions, visit
academic.cengage.com.

Purchase any of our products at your local college store or at our
preferred online store **www.ichapters.com.**

Printed in the United States of America
1 2 3 4 5 6 7 12 11 10 09 08

To the partnership
that brought this book about

and

to Miles, R.J., Sasha, Matthew, and Brendan
whose promise shines

About the Authors

Ralph L. Rosnow, an emeritus professor at Temple University in Philadelphia, PA, has also taught courses in research methods and social psychology at Boston University and Harvard University and has authored and coauthored many books and articles in these content areas. Visit the author's Web site at http://rosnow.socialpsychology.org. **Mimi Rosnow,** with a background in English, has done freelance editorial consulting, and for a number of years was an editorial assistant at a national magazine.

Brief Contents

Contents

CHAPTER SEVEN **Writing and Polishing**   **77**

CHAPTER EIGHT **Producing the Final Manuscript**   **97**

Exhibits

Preface for Instructors

This eighth edition of *Writing Papers in Psychology* provides frameworks, tips, guidelines, and sample illustrations for college students who are writing research reports or literature reviews that are expected to conform to style recommendations in the fifth edition of the *Publication Manual of the American Psychological Association* (hereafter called the *APA Manual*). Chapter 1 contains a flowchart (Exhibit 1) that walks the student through all phases of these two projects as well as the proposal and, if required, a poster and a concise report of the research for distribution. *Writing Papers* is intended to be more than just an APA style guide, however. It is designed to cultivate organizing, literature retrieval, critical reasoning, and communication skills under deadlines. For students who do not plan to continue in psychology, the APA style may have little relevance after the baccalaureate, but these other skills should be relevant for a lifetime.

Nonetheless, with a few exceptions, the sample materials conform to the APA style. One exception is the title page of the final review or research paper. The *APA Manual* calls student papers *final manuscripts* because they reach their audience (in this case, the instructor) exactly as they are prepared, whereas papers submitted for publication are *copy manuscripts* that are useful only until they have gone to the typesetter. The title pages of the final manuscripts in appendixes A and B contain information of relevance to the instructor. The title page of a copy manuscript intended for submission to a journal provides information needed by the journal editor and the typesetter. To illustrate this difference, Exhibit 12 shows what a cover page for a copy manuscript in APA style looks like, including the *running head*, which is absent in the student papers. The running head is an abbreviated title that is proposed for the top of each page in the published articles of APA journals, though not all APA journals actually use running heads (e.g., *American Psychologist*).

Several exhibits that were in the previous edition of *Writing Papers* have been dropped and some new ones (Exhibit 12) added. There is a new exhibit illustrating how clustering can be used to begin to focus the first draft of a review paper (Exhibit 10). The examples of referencing in APA style (in chapter 8) are now numbered, and Exhibit 14 provides a mini-table-of-contents of those examples. In 1999, the APA's Task Force on Statistical Inference recommended ways of improving the reporting of statistical information, such as reporting interval estimates for means, proportions, and effect sizes.[1] The sample poster

---

[1]L. Wilkinson and Task Force on Statistical Inference (1999). Statistical methods in psychology journals: Guidelines and explanations, *American Psychologist, 54*, 594–604.

(Exhibit 17) shows a histogram emphasizing group means and 95% confidence intervals, and at the end of chapter 6, all the recommended readings are in the spirit of the APA Task Force recommendations.

Chapter 2 on finding and using reference sources has been revised and tightened to provide a greater emphasis on electronic retrieval of reference materials. Not neglected, but more focused, is the discussion of essential print resources in the college library. The illustration of how a student might use PsycINFO® (and InfoTrac® College Edition) has been updated. We again note the rules of library etiquette, and in this edition of *Writing Papers* we also mention the importance of e-mail etiquette. There is also an emphasis on careful note-taking, citing and referencing work properly, and the avoidance of plagiarism and lazy writing. There are many other changes in this edition of *Writing Papers* designed to increase its timeliness and user friendliness.

In chapter 6, we continue to emphasize that, when reporting statistical information, it be done clearly, accurately, precisely, and in enough detail to allow readers to reach their own conclusions. Though the APA Task Force on Statistical Inference underscored the limitations of the rhetoric of the accept/reject paradigm in null hypothesis significance testing, researchers have been slow to embrace those recommendations, possibly because of entrenched habits as well as inconsistencies in the APA Publication Manual.[2] For example, the *APA Manual* cautions against the reporting of "multiple degree-of-freedom effect indicators" (p. 26), but illustrates an ANOVA table (p. 162) in which six out of seven effect sizes are multiple degree-of-freedom indicators based on omnibus F tests. The rule of thumb used in *Writing Papers* is to report effect sizes only in association with focused statistical tests (e.g., F tests with numerator $df = 1$, any t test, or any 1-df chi-square), a practice that is illustrated in the research report in appendix A.

In reporting quantitative values, students are often puzzled by how many decimal places to indicate. The *APA Manual's* rule of thumb is to report descriptive data (e.g., means, standard deviations, Cohen's d) and inferential test results (e.g., t, F, chi-square) to two decimal places—which is the standard used in *Writing Papers*. In computing statistical results by hand, however, problems could arise if the student scrimped on the number of decimal places in the intermediate calculations, as rounding errors could produce inaccurate results. To emphasize this point, all of the intermediate calculations indicated in the appendix section of the sample research report are not rounded to two decimal places (though scientific calculators and computers do not round until the end anyway).

Students also frequently ask how to report statistical significance, particularly when they see statements like "significant difference" and "no significant difference" but no indication of the actual p value. Statements like these can

---

[2]F. Fidler, N. Thomason, G. Cumming, S. Finch, & J. Leeman, (2004). Editors can lead researchers to confidence intervals, but can't make them think: Statistical reform lessons from medicine. *Psychological Science, 15,* 119–126.

be terribly misleading if all the writer means is that the obtained p value was on the "wrong" side of .05. There is something absurd about regarding as a "real effect" one that is supported by $p = .05$ and as a "zero effect" one that is supported by $p = .06$. The sample research report shows the tabular values to two decimal places, and shows the p values more precisely indicated in the results section (using scientific notation to compress the number of decimal places). Chapter 6 provides further guidance while also cautioning students about avoiding the traps of false precision and needless precision in reporting results. Added to the list of readings is Peter R. Killeen's article on p_{rep}, as the APS journal *Psychological Science* recommends this statistic.

Acknowledgments

We thank two outstanding psychology teachers, Anne A. Skleder (Chatham University) and Bruce Rind (Temple University), for earlier versions of the sample papers, which we have reworked in different editions of *Writing Papers*; we especially thank Dr. Rind for the raw data in the research report, which are empirical data that he collected. We also thank another outstanding teacher, Eric K. Foster (Temple University and Wharton School of Business), for the literature retrieval experience launching chapter 2 ("Maya" is the name of Dr. Foster's daughter). We thank Marion Harrell of the American Psychological Association for her suggestions for updates of our discussion of PsycINFO and its companion resources. We are grateful to Erik Evans, our editor at Wadsworth, for his enthusiasm and support. Once again, we thank Margaret Ritchie for her skillful editing.

We thank the following reviewers of the seventh edition of *Writing Papers* for comments and suggestions that were enormously helpful to us in writing this eighth edition: Stanley Cohen (West Virginia University); Laura Levine (Central Connecticut State University); Holly M. Schiffrin (University of Mary Washington); and Linda M. Subich (University of Akron). We again thank the following people, whose comments and suggestions improved one or more previous editions of *Writing Papers*: John B. Best (Eastern Illinois University); Thomas Brown (Utica College of Syracuse University); David E. Campbell (Humboldt State University); Scott D. Churchill (University of Dallas); Peter B. Crabb (Penn State University-Abington); Nicholas DiFonzo (Rochester Institute of Technology); Nancy Eldred (San Jose State University); Kenneth Elliott (University of Maine at Augusta); Robert Gallen (Georgetown College); David Goldstein (Duke University); John Hall (Texas Wesleyan University); Donald Hantula (Temple University); James W. Kalat (North Carolina State University); Allan J. Kimmel (Groupe École Supérieure de Commerce de Paris, France); Arlene Lundquist (Mount Union College); Joann Montepare (Tufts University); Quentin Newhouse, Jr. (Bowie State University); Ben Newkirk (Grossmont College); Arthur Nonneman (Asbury College); Edgar O'Neal (Tulane University); Rick Pollack (Merrimack College); Maureen Powers (Vanderbilt University); MaryLu Rosenthal

(Riverside, CA); Robert Rosenthal (University of California at Riverside); Gordon W. Russell (University of Lethbridge, Canada); Helen Shoemaker (California State University at Hayward); John Sparrow (State University of New York at Geneseo); Claudia Stanny (University of West Florida); David B. Strohmetz (Monmouth University); Stephen A. Truhon (Winston-Salem State University); Lori Van Wallendael (University of North Carolina).

Finally, we thank the many users of *Writing Papers*. Your suggestions have helped us to improve each new edition. We again invite instructors and students to send us recommendations for further improvements (http://rosnow.socialpsychology.org).

Ralph and Mimi Rosnow

1

Getting Started

Writing papers to fulfill course requirements means knowing what the instructor expects and then formulating a plan to accomplish your goal on schedule. This chapter will help you get started. It also includes some simple dos and don'ts to help you avoid pitfalls and to ensure that the assignment will be completed on time and that it will represent your best work.

Where to Begin

There was once an intriguing character named Joe Gould, who, after graduating from Harvard in 1911 and trying his hand at a number of futile endeavors, moved to New York City and began to hang around Greenwich Village coffee shops. He told people that he had mastered the language of seagulls—and, in fact, did an uncanny imitation of one—and was translating literature into "seagull." He was best known, however, for an ambitious project he claimed to be compiling, called the "Oral History of Our Times." He boasted of having accumulated a stack of notebooks that stood 7 feet tall, and he carried brown paper bags with him that, he said, contained research notes. Joe Gould died in a psychiatric hospital while doing his seagull imitation. Some years later, in a profile article written by Joseph Mitchell for the *New Yorker* magazine, it was revealed that Joe Gould never started his "Oral History"; his notebooks were a myth, and his brown bags contained merely other bags and yellowed newspaper clippings.

For students with required writing assignments, Joe Gould is a metaphor for the most challenging aspect of any project: how to get started. First of all, familiarize yourself with what is in this book. Exhibit 1 shows a flowchart referring to specific chapters and selections that you can turn to as needed. The table of contents (at the beginning of this book) shows the specialized sections and their location in each chapter, and immediately following the table of contents is a list of exhibits. The index (at the back of the book) lists specific terms, should you

EXHIBIT 1   Flowchart to walk you through Writing Papers

Find out what is expected, and start formulating your ideas and getting organized. (Chapter 1)

↓

Find the detailed information you're going to need for your literature review or the key studies you're going to need for your research proposal. (Chapter 2)

↓

Write the proposal. (Chapter 3) →

If you did empirical research (appendix A) and are ready to put your ideas and results together, familiarize yourself with the traditional structure. (Chapter 4)

↓

If you are writing a review paper (appendix B) and are ready to organize your thinking, develop an outline for the first draft. (Chapter 5)

↓

Be prepared to report statistical information clearly, accurately, precisely, and in enough detail so that others are able to reach their own conclusions. (Chapter 6)

↓

If you are reporting quantitative information, be prepared to do so clearly, accurately, precisely, and in enough detail so that others are able to reach their own conclusions. (Chapter 6)

↓

Begin writing the first draft. (Chapter 7)

↓

Begin writing the first draft. (Chapter 7)

↓

Revise and polish your writing, and prepare the final manuscript for submission to the instructor. (Chapter 8)

↓

Revise and polish your writing, and prepare the final manuscript for submission to the instructor. (Chapter 8)

↓

If you are presenting a poster or handing out a brief report, use the sample material as a reference point. (Chapter 9) need to find a particular topic. There are also sample materials through-out. Chapter 3 contains two sample proposals, one for a literature review (Exhibit 6) and the other for a research project (Exhibit 7). Near the end of the book are two appendixes (tabbed, so that they're easier to find). Appendix A shows a final research report (Jane Doe's), and appendix B, a final review paper (John Smith's). There is a sample poster presentation (Exhibits 16 and 17) and a sample one-page, two-sided handout (Exhibit 18) in chapter 9, both based on Jane Doe's research project.

Not everything that appears in the sample papers in appendixes A and B will be needed in every student paper, but anything you might need is illustrated there or elsewhere in this book. If your assignment is to write a review of a single empirical study, your paper will not be nearly as long or as detailed as John Smith's literature review in appendix B. Your final review of a single empirical study might be only three to five pages long. If your assignment is to write a lab report in an experimental psychology class, your report will not be as long or detailed as Jane Doe's report of original research in appendix A. Even if your required writing assignment is different from John's or Jane's, read both papers anyway because we refer to them throughout this book, and you may get some ideas for your own writing assignment. They also show what a student paper written in "APA style" looks like.

Writing in APA Style

The term *APA style* means that the structure and format of a manuscript are consistent with the guidelines in the fifth edition of the *Publication Manual of the American Psychological Association* (called the *APA Manual* in this book). Writing in APA style is what college instructors in psychology typi-cally require of students, although it is not the only writing style that you may encounter in college. In English, language, and literature classes, instructors often require students to write "research papers" in a style recommended by the Modern Language Association (called *MLA style*). In that context, the term *research paper* also means something quite different from Jane Doe's research paper in appendix A. In an English class, you will be "researching the literature" for your paper, whereas in psychology, a *research paper* means you will be writing up the results of an empirical study. You will also be doing some "researching" of the literature for your proposal, but this process is called "searching and retrieving" in this book. Incidentally, the APA style and the MLA style are not the only two styles for the structure and format of manuscripts; there are also the University of Chicago style, the Turabian style, *The New York Times* style, *The Wall Street Journal* style, and so on.[1]

---

[1]To get you used to the idea that there are other writing styles besides the APA style, we use footnotes for reference citations in this book. It is not unusual to see footnotes in technical books that do not use APA style; the author uses them so as not to interrupt the flow of a sentence with multiple parenthetical citations. Of course, the citations and references in the sample papers (appendixes A and B) are all in APA style.

Although we said that both Jane Doe's and John Smith's final papers are in APA style, there are actually some departures from the *APA Manual*. We will have more to say about these departures, but the difference has to do with student papers' being thought of as *final manuscripts* rather than *copy manuscripts*. As described in the *APA Manual*, copy manuscripts are specifically written for editors, reviewers, and typesetters. Once a copy manuscript has been accepted for publication and has gone through the production process, it is discarded. Papers written by students for class assignments are in a final form for the instructor to read. The same is true of theses and dissertations, which are also considered final manuscripts even when the audience is not only the student's adviser or mentor. Another important point is that, as the *APA Manual* cautions, style preferences for some student manuscripts may be diverse and often specific to a particular institution. If you are writing a thesis or a dissertation, check with your department for any special style requirements, and ask your adviser to recommend a couple of examples that will give you a sense of what is considered quality work.

The American Psychological Association sells software called the *APA Style Helper,* which is designed for Microsoft Word on Windows (see http://apastyle.apa.org). Depending on the textbook you have been assigned in the class in which you are writing a paper, the publisher probably also has a Web site with information and online links. There are reliable free Web sites with information about APA style, such as http://www.docstyles.com/apacrib.htm, where you will find Russ Dewey and Abel Scribe's *APA Research Style Crib Sheet,* which is a synopsis of APA style rules. There is also http://www.wisc.edu/writing/Handbook/DocAPAPrinciples.html, which is a site created by the Writing Center at the University of Wisconsin-Madison. Templates that you fill in with reference information to see how a citation or a reference should look in APA style can be found at http://citationmachine.net/index.php?source=58&callstyle=2&all=#here, a very helpful Web site created by David Warlick.

Your Instructor's Expectations

To plan your project, you need some clear objectives and a precise idea of what your instructor expects of you. For example, what is the purpose of the writing assignment, and how long should the final paper be? Do you choose the theme or topic, or will the instructor assign it? Will interim papers (for example, a proposal and progress reports) be required; how long should they be, and when are they due? When is the final paper due, and how does this date mesh with your other assignments (for example, exams and papers in other courses)? You can speak with other students about their impressions, but the person who knows *exactly* what is expected of you is the instructor. Before you boot up your computer or sharpen any pencils, meet with the instructor, articulate what you understand the assignment to be, talk about your ideas for a topic, and ask if you are on the right path.

One instructor wrote to us that many of his students were reluctant to take this initial step, even though they hadn't a clue about a topic for a required research project. But those who did come in, even without an initial idea, benefited from the meeting and, in most cases, went away with at least the beginning of a direction for their work. Meeting with the instructor will also give you an opportunity to avoid the anonymity of being just another face in the classroom. The instructor knows who are, and that you are a motivated student. If you decide to go on to graduate school, you have introduced yourself to someone you may wish to approach later on to ask for a recommendation letter.

Focusing on Your Objective

Once you have a topic, think through the assignment to sharpen your intellectual process. Understanding the differences between the research report and the review paper in psychology classes will help you focus on your particular objective. There are, as we said, reports of lab exercises and reviews of single studies, but for this discussion we will concentrate on the general types exemplified by Jane Doe's research report in appendix A and John Smith's literature review paper in appendix B. Let's start with the typical differences between the research report and the review paper (see Exhibit 2), so you can focus your efforts on whichever project you have been assigned.

One obvious distinction highlighted in Exhibit 2 is that a literature search forms the core of the review paper, and empirical data form the core of the research report. Empirical research generally requires a preliminary literature review, but it typically involves retrieving only a few key studies that will serve as theoretical starting points. To give you an idea of how this review might be

EXHIBIT 2   *Differences between research reports and review papers*

Research Report	*Review Paper*
1. Is based on data that you have collected; literature search involving only a few key studies.	1. Is based exclusively on literature search; no hard data of your own to interpret, unless you are counting and summarizing the information.
2. Is structured to follow the traditional form described in chapter 4.	2. Is structured by you to fit your particular topic, based on an outline you prepared (described in chapter 5).
3. Reports your own research findings and conclusions to others in enough detail so they can draw their own conclusions.	3. Puts the literature you review into the context of your own insights to bring coherence to the material.

done, chapter 2 begins with an example. The point, however, is that you can expect to spend more time retrieving abstracts and articles online, and probably more time reading and taking notes, if you are writing a review paper. On the other hand, if you are writing a review of a single empirical study, you may not need to do much of a literature search for just a 3- to 5-page paper. However, in some upper-level undergraduate seminars that are run like graduate courses, the instructor may expect a 25- to 30-page final paper with a literature review similar in detail and a cohesive argument to those in John Smith's paper in appendix B.

In some review papers the author reports the results of having counted and quantitatively summarized information. When this counting and quantifying involves a statistical analysis of the results from numerous studies for the purpose of integrating the findings, the review is called a *meta-analysis*. In psychology and biomedicine, meta-analytic reviews are becoming increasingly popular because they take stock of empirical findings that address essentially the same research question. If you are interested in seeing what a meta-analytic review looks like, you will find examples in the journal *Psychological Bulletin*. Usually, such a review describes (a) the typical magnitude of observed effects (called the *effect sizes*); (b) their variability (i.e., how spread out the observed effects are); (c) their *p* values (their levels of statistical significance); and (d) the variables that can predict the relative magnitude of the observed effects (called *moderator variables*). For more about meta-analysis and effect sizes, see the recommended readings at the end of chapter 6.

Notice in the opening line of the introduction section of John Smith's literature review that he cites an encyclopedia article. A lot of material is available online, some in full text (discussed in the next chapter), but some material is available only in the library, such as the encyclopedia that John consulted and took notes from. Perusing the stacks (the shelves throughout the library) might just turn up something interesting and unexpected. You might find a shelf full of psychology encyclopedias or a classic work that you have heard about. If you are writing a senior thesis or a master's thesis, you will be expected to do more just than a cursory search of the literature; we will show how in the next chapter.

A second distinction in Exhibit 2 is that the structure of the research report is expected to conform to a general tradition that has evolved over many years. As a consequence, instructors expect research reports to typically include (a) an abstract, (b) an introduction, (c) a method section, (d) a results section, (e) a discussion of the results, and (f) a list of the references cited. Jane Doe's research report in appendix A contains some additional material, but you will be expected to include at least these six parts. If you open an APA research journal, you will see examples of this basic structure. Review papers, on the other hand, are much more flexible, because it is not always immediately evident, even to experienced writers, how the final manuscript will take shape until they have had an opportunity to think about everything in more than just a piecemeal fashion.

To give a sense of the flexibility of review papers, Duke University psychologist Harris M. Cooper described the following objectives and categories:[2]

◆ The *focus* of the literature review concerns the material on which the reviewer wants to concentrate his or her attention, although there may be more than one focal point in the review. Literature reviews in psychology tend to focus on research outcomes, research methods, theories, or practices and applications. In John Smith's proposal (Exhibit 6 in chapter 3), he states that his literature review will focus on "two theoretical orientations regarding the nature of human intelligence."

◆ The *goal* is what the reviewer hopes to achieve, which usually is to integrate a body of related work by formulating a general statement, resolving conflicting ideas, or bridging the gap between theories by proposing a common linguistic framework. A second goal is to critically analyze the existing literature, and a third is to identify central issues. John Smith proposes a term—*multiplex*—to conceptually integrate different approaches to the idea of distinct types of intelligence besides the *g*-centered type (in appendix B).

◆ The *perspective* is the point of view influencing the discussion, which for simplicity is called either a *neutral representation* or the *espousal of a position*. John's final paper in appendix B is a distillation of ideas expressed in a relatively detached tone.

◆ The *coverage* is what primarily distinguishes one literature review from another, because reviewers search the literature and make decisions about the suitability of material based on their own specified criteria. Generally speaking, the coverage might be exhaustive, exhaustive with selective citation, representative, or central and pivotal. John's review is representative with selective citations that are specifically addressed to the focus of the coverage.

◆ The *organization* of the literature review is how the material cited is arranged, for example, historically, conceptually, or methodologically. John's review amalgamates the conceptual and methodological arrangement, and he also gives a flavor of the history of the intelligence-testing movement.

◆ The intended *audience* is the target group to which the review is addressed. The group might be specialized scholars, general scholars, practitioners and policy makers, or the public at large. For John, the audience is the instructor, assumed to be a scholar with general and specialized knowledge and interests.

The final distinction noted in Exhibit 2 is that the review paper puts issues and ideas into the context of a particular theme or thesis, whereas the main objective of the research report is to describe your empirical investigation to others.

---

[2]H. M. Cooper (1988). Organizing knowledge syntheses: A taxonomy of literature reviews. *Knowledge in Society: The International Journal of Knowledge Transfer, 1,* 104–126.

The theme in a research report often involves testable hypotheses with explicit predictions, but the report could be an exploratory study or a purely descriptive investigation (there is more on these distinctions later in this book). If there are hypotheses, then what you found in your research should be put in the context of the predictions, as in the results and discussion sections of Jane Doe's research report in appendix A.

Scheduling Time

Once you have a clear sense of your objective, the next step is to set some deadlines so you do not end up like Joe Gould, who was so paralyzed by inertia that he accomplished nothing. You know your own energy level and thought patterns, so play to your strengths. Are you a morning person? If so, block out some time to work on your writing early in the day. Do you function better at night? Then use the late hours of quiet to your advantage. Allow extra time for other pursuits by setting realistic dates by which you can reasonably expect to complete each major part of your assignment. Write the dates on your calendar; some students prefer to post the dates over their desks as daily reminders.

In planning your schedule, give yourself ample time to do a good job. Patience will pay off by making you feel more confident as you complete each task and move on to the next one. How do you know what tasks to schedule? Because writing a literature review requires spending time online (and also probably in the library) finding sources, reading them, and accumulating your notes, you will need to leave ample time for these tasks. Here are some ideas about what to schedule on your calendar if you are writing a review paper and are first required to submit a proposal:

◆ Completion of preliminary literature search for proposal
◆ Completion of proposal
◆ Completion of literature search
◆ Completion of library work
◆ Completion of an outline and first draft
◆ Completion of final draft and proofing

If you are writing a research report based on an empirical investigation, you need to set aside time for the ethics review, the implementation of the research, and the data analysis. Here are some scheduling suggestions for these and other tasks if you will be doing empirical research and are first required to submit a proposal:

◆ Completion of preliminary literature search for proposal
◆ Completion of proposal for research
◆ Completion of ethics review
◆ Implementation of the study
◆ Completion of data analysis
◆ Completion of an outline and first draft
◆ Completion of final draft and proofing

Both schedules of tasks should allow time between the first and final drafts so that you can distance yourself from your writing. Organizing, writing, and revising will take time. A book or a journal article you need might be unavailable. Data collection and analysis can also run into snags. Other problems might be that the ethics review takes longer than you expected, or you are asked to resubmit your proposal, or your research subjects do not cooperate, or a computer you need is down, or research material you need is hard to find. In your schedule, allow yourself time to cope with unforeseen problems like these and time to return to your writing assignment with a fresh perspective as you polish the first draft and check for errors in logic, flow, spelling, punctuation, and grammar. By scheduling your time in this way, you should not feel pressured by an imaginary deadline—or surprised as the real deadline approaches.

If you get started early, you will also have time to track down hard-to-find material or to locate a test you need. If you want to use a specific test protected by copyright, getting permission to use the test will take time. Although tests that require advanced training to administer or interpret are usually unavailable to undergraduates, many others are available to students. There are general reference books that contain sample measures, and you can ask a reference librarian for suggestions on how to identify and locate these books in the library. For a comprehensive catalog of available tests and measures that you can look up in journal articles and reports, see the *Directory of Unpublished Experimental Mental Measures,* a series edited by Bert A. Goldman, David F. Mitchell, and others (published by the American Psychological Association); the "unpublished" in the title means that the instrument is generally available without a fee or special credentials. A huge online database (created by Evelyn and Linda Perloff) is Health and Psychosocial Instruments (HaPI), available on the Ovid database; it includes questionnaires, checklists, rating scales, interview schedules, and specialized tests for use in research. Your instructor will also be able to provide you with other good leads.

Should you encounter a problem, discuss it early with the instructor to ensure that you can finish on schedule. Starting early may also give you time to tackle data analysis procedures that are not in the course textbook. You might also want to e-mail a researcher and request any follow-up articles that are still unpublished, if you think you need them, or to request permission to reprint or reproduce something. In John Smith's paper in appendix B (see John's Author Note), he acknowledges that he received permission to reproduce a graphic. He also thanks the instructor for directing him to a graduate-level text he consulted about a statistical point she brought up. Jane Doe had to get permission from the restaurant owner and the server to conduct her experiment, and she needed ample time to do the data analyses described in the appendix of her report.

Another word of advice: Instructors have heard all the possible excuses for a late or badly done final term paper, so don't expect much sympathy if you miss the final deadline. If you expect to ask the instructor for a letter of recommendation for graduate school or a job, you certainly don't want to create the impression that you are unreliable.

Choosing a Topic

The next step is to come up with a research idea or choose a suitable topic for a literature review. The selection of a research idea or review topic is an integral part of learning, because usually you are free to explore experiences, observations, and ideas for questions or issues that will sustain your curiosity and interest as you work on your project. There are lots of ways of getting ideas. For example, John notes in his proposal for a literature review (Exhibit 6 in chapter 3) that he first became interested in the idea of multiple intelligences when the instructor in his psychological testing course mentioned her own research on a facet of that work. Jane Doe, in her proposal for a research study (Exhibit 7 in chapter 3), describes a similar situation and notes her personal interest in the topic she would like to study.

If you are a psychology major or minor, you probably already have lots of questions and ideas regarding why people behave, perceive, or think as they do. But if you are looking around for an idea, and your psychology department invites guest researchers to present colloquiums that are open to undergraduate students (most usually are), take a pencil and paper to jot down any ideas you get. You may also have an opportunity to ask the speaker a question; listen to others' questions, too, and the speaker's responses, and if there is an open reception afterward, chat with the speaker. Another way to stimulate your creative mind is to peruse the journals in some specialty area that interests you, and to look again at the texts in the courses that you enjoyed. Approaching this material with an open, inquisitive mind is likely to stimulate creative thinking. However, if you cannot come up with an idea, discuss your dilemma with the instructor and ask for advice.

In considering a suitable topic, beware of a few pitfalls. The following are dos and don'ts that might make your life easier as you start choosing a topic:

- ◆ Do choose a topic that piques your curiosity and will sustain your interest over the long haul.
- ◆ Do make sure your topic can be covered in the available time and in the assigned number of pages.
- ◆ Don't choose a topic that you know other students have chosen; you will be competing with them for access to the library's source material.
- ◆ If you are not already knowledgeable on a topic, do read about it before you try to narrow your topic.

Narrowing the Topic

Choosing too broad or too narrow a topic for either a literature review or a research project will add difficulties and anxiety and will mean an unsatisfactory result. A proposed review that is too broad—for example, "Sigmund Freud's Life and Times"—would try to cover too much material within the limited framework of the assignment and the time available to complete it. A specific aspect of Freud's theoretical work (assuming you are interested in psychoanalytic writings) will prove a more appropriately narrowed focus for a review paper in a course on personality theories, abnormal behavior, or psychopathology.

In narrowing the literature review topic, do not limit your discussion just to facts that are already well known. Ask yourself what is special about how you plan to approach the assignment. For example, John Smith's review paper is not just a listing of other people's conclusions, but an effort to incorporate his own perspective. This approach not only will give the project a specific focus but will also make the paper stand out when the instructor grades it. Here are two further guidelines in narrowing your topic:

◆ Be sure that your topic is not so narrow that reference materials will be hard to find.
◆ Be guided by your instructor's advice because the instructor can help you avoid taking on an unwieldy topic.

If you approach instructors with several concrete ideas, you will usually find them glad to help tailor those ideas so that you, the topic, and the project format are compatible. Here are examples of how a student who is assigned a review paper might sharpen the focus of a paper on Sigmund Freud:

Unlimited Topic (Much Too Broad)
"To examine Freud's theories of personality and abnormal behavior"

Limited to 20-Page Paper
"To examine Freud's theory of Oedipal conflict applied to mental health"

Limited to 10-Page Paper
"To examine Freud's theory of infantile sexuality"

Here is another example of concentrating the student's focus, in this case for a one- or two-semester research project:

Unlimited Topic (Too Broad for a Term Project)
"To investigate how nonverbal stimuli are deciphered"

Slightly Limited Topic
"To investigate how certain kinds of nonverbal stimuli are deciphered differently by women and men"

Adequately Limited Topic
"To investigate whether female and male volunteer subjects at Podunk U. differ in their ability to identify photographed facial expressions of joy, disappointment, anger, and fear in a sample of female and male actors"

If you are currently enrolled in a research methods course, the assigned text probably discusses criteria for assessing the merits of good scientific hypotheses. A detailed discussion is beyond the scope of this book, but we can mention three criteria:

1. *Good hypotheses are plausible, or credible.* That is, they are grounded in credible ideas and facts, the assumption being that well-grounded hypotheses will have a high payoff potential when tested. In other words, you must do a preliminary literature search to find out whether your ideas are consistent with accepted findings in the scientific literature. If they are not, then you will need to think about the inconsistencies and decide (with the help of the instructor) whether you really have a fresh insight or will need to develop some other hypothesis.

2. *Good hypotheses are succinct, logically coherent, and consistent with the facts, and technical terms are used correctly and precisely.* To see whether you are using a technical term correctly, consult the *APA Dictionary of Psychology* or an encyclopedia of psychology (or whatever area you are interested in), but don't just rely on a lazy online search. To ensure that your hypothesis is succinct and coherent, consult your instructor, who will show you how to cut away unwieldy words. This word-trimming and focusing process is known as using "Occam's razor"—named after a 14th-century Franciscan philosopher, William of Ockham, who cautioned against wordy explanations that can be stated more succinctly.

3. *Good hypotheses are testable, and they are empirically falsifiable if incorrect.* Since anyone with a fertile imagination can concoct support for even the most preposterous belief, the idea is that hypotheses that cannot be refuted by *any* means are not within the realm of science. For example, the statement "All behavior is a product of the good and evil lying within us" does not qualify as a valid scientific hypothesis, because it is so vague and amorphous that it cannot be subjected to empirical refutation.

Knowing Your Audience and Topic

All professional writers know that they are writing for a particular audience. This knowledge helps them determine the tone and style of their work. Think of a journalist's report of a house fire and contrast it with a short story describing the same event. Knowing one's audience is no less important when the writer is a college student and the project is a literature review or a research report. The audience is your instructor, who is not just any reader, but someone knowledgeable in the area. Thus, you are writing to demonstrate your own acquired knowledge and also to give evidence of your insights and ability to express your ideas plausibly, coherently, logically, and persuasively to this sophisticated reader.

If you have questions about the instructor's grading criteria, find out what they are before you start to work. For example, in a course on research methods, one instructor's syllabus listed the following grading criteria for different parts of the finished report (the numbers in parentheses are percentages):

Abstract
    Informativeness (5)
Introduction
    Clarity of purpose (10)
    Literature review (10)
Method
    Adequacy of design (10)
    Quality and completeness of description (10)
Results
    Appropriateness and correctness of analysis (10)
    Use of tables or figures (5)
    Clarity of presentation (10)
Discussion
    Interpretation of results (10)
    Critique/future directions (10)
Miscellaneous
    Organization, style, references, etc. (5)
    Appendix for raw data and calculations (5)

This information enabled the students to concentrate on different parts of the assignment just as the instructor would concentrate on them when evaluating the reports. This information can also serve as a checklist for you to make sure that everything of importance is covered in your finished report. Not every instructor will provide such detailed information about grading practices, but this manual can help you develop your own personal checklist based on other information the instructor has provided.

Cultivating an Understanding

Let us assume that you know what your main audience—your instructor—expects of you. Now you must try to develop more than a superficial understanding of your topic. The more you read about it and discuss your ideas with friends, the more you will begin to cultivate an intuitive understanding of the topic. In the next chapter, we describe how to use computerized and library resources to nurture this understanding. Here are two tips to get you started:

◆ Some writers find it helpful to keep several 3 × 5-inch cards handy, or to use sticky notes, for jotting down relevant ideas that suddenly occur to them. This is a good way to keep your topic squarely in your mind.
◆ You need to understand your source material, so equip yourself with a good desk dictionary, and turn to it routinely whenever you come across an unfamiliar word. This habit will serve you well. If you plan to continue in psychology, having your own copy of the *APA Dictionary of Psychology* will be helpful (see www.apa.org/books).

The most comprehensive dictionaries in your college library are labeled *unabridged* (that is, they have not been condensed by the omission of terms or definitions). The most famous (and most comprehensive) of all unabridged dictionaries in the English language is the multivolume *Oxford English Dictionary* (called for short the *OED*). Some libraries provide electronic access to the OED. If you are that rare student who loves obscure origins of words, the OED is the place to look.

2

Finding and Using Reference Materials

The literature search is an indispensable step in preparing a review paper; it is also an essential aspect of a research proposal as it puts your own ideas in context, building on the existing work of others. Knowing about the many online and print resources available will allow you to gauge the effort it will take to find the information you need. If you know how to retrieve this information electronically, you can save time and effort.

Looking Over Maya's Shoulder

Let us assume you have an idea for a research project or a review paper, have spoken about it in a preliminary way with your instructor, and know that you must produce a written proposal. In the next chapter, we illustrate the nature of the proposal. Before you begin drafting it, however, you will need to identify and read relevant work on the topic in which you are interested. To help you, we begin by looking over the shoulder of a student, named Maya, who wants to gather a few key studies to help her formulate one or two hypotheses and write a proposal for a research project. First, we describe how Maya goes through the step-by-step process of doing a literature search. Afterward, we will examine in more detail the resources she used and others that may be available in college libraries or electronically through their Web sites. (For a list of definitions of common terms and jargon used on the Web, see Exhibit 3. For a more extensive glossary, go to http://www.lib.berkeley.edu/TeachingLib/Guides/Internet/Glossary.html.)

Maya thinks she wants to study a spin-off from the instructor's lecture on what he called the "Pygmalion experiment," a classic research study by Robert Rosenthal and Lenore Jacobson. In a book the instructor mentioned, called *Pygmalion in the Classroom*, Rosenthal and Jacobson described how, in the 1960s, they had given a standard nonverbal intelligence test to the

EXHIBIT 3   *Common terms and jargon on the Web*

attachment: a digitally coded file that is downloaded when you specifically open an add-on to an e-mail message; the attachment might contain words, images, or, in a worst case scenario, a hidden virus.

browser: a program that is used to display Web pages.

cache: a place on the computer's hard drive where images and text from visited Web pages are stored to speed up the process of downloading the next time they are visited. Caches can, however, clutter the hard drive, particularly when information on the Web pages is constantly updated, so it is a good idea to clean the cache occasionally.

cookies: bits of personalized information left on the hard drive by some Web sites so they can track visitors online (some Web sites will not admit visitors unless they agree to accept a cookie). There are cookie cleanup programs to send this clutter into oblivion.

database: a collection of data, such as the reference databases shown in Exhibit 5.

firewall: a system that protects online computers from outside hackers who want to steal information or create a launching pad for destructive signals to Web sites.

full-text database: textual material that can be electronically perused in its entirety, such as the complete content of a journal article, a book, a dictionary, or an encyclopedia.

html: the coded language (Hypertext Markup Language) used to create Web pages.

http: acronym for Hypertext Transfer Protocol, the prefix (http://) of many URLs; it signifies how computers communicate with one another on the Internet.

hyperlink: a coded image (an icon or a button) or a coded word or phrase (usually in blue and underlined) that changes to a hand when you move your mouse pointer over it; clicking the hyperlink transports you to another place.

Internet service provider: the company or organization providing access to the Internet.

JPEG: acronym for Joint Photographic Experts Group, which is the most popular format on the Internet for photos because it supports 24-bit color and subtle variations in brightness and hue.

online search: the use of a computer and a search engine to retrieve information.

PDF: acronym for Portable Document Format, PDF retains the look of the original document and is viewed by means of the Acrobat Reader installed on your computer (or available free from http://www.adobe.com).

search engine: a program (such as Google or Yahoo or MSN) that takes key words, queries an internal index, and returns a set of Web documents. Usually, if you click on "Help," you will find search help instructions, terminology, and advanced search tips.

spam: unsolicited e-mail that is automatically sent to all those on an address list.

URL: acronym for Uniform Resource Locator, which is another name for the Web address. The URL of a helpful Web site that was created at the University of Waterloo and that contains links to national and international psychological societies (including the American Psychological Association and the American Psychological Society, which post information about student funding and career planning), is http://www.lib.uwaterloo.ca/society/psychol_soc.html. If you are interested in the field of social psychology, you might check the Social Psychology Network at http://www.socialpsychology.org, created at Wesleyan University by Dr. Scott Plous.

viruses: damaging codes that invade a computer's hard drive when an infected attachment or a contaminated file is opened. Some viruses, called *worms,* copy themselves and spread rapidly in the hard drive; others, called *Trojan horses,* assume the appearance of normal files but secretly wipe the hard drive clean. As a safeguard against viruses, be cautious about what you download or open, and install (and routinely update, usually weekly) antivirus software to check attachments before you open them and, in a worst case scenario, to find and try to repair damage to your hard drive.

children in a public elementary school in South San Francisco. The teachers were told only that the test was one of intellectual "blooming," and approximately 20% of the children (whose names the investigators had picked at random) were represented to the teachers as capable of marked intellectual growth based on their performance on this test. In other words, the difference between the supposed potential bloomers and the other students existed solely in the minds of their teachers. The children's performance on the intelligence test was measured after one semester, again after a full academic year, and again after two academic years. The results revealed that, although the greatest differential gain in total intelligence appeared after one school year, the bloomers held an advantage over the other children even after two years. Maya's instructor described these results as an example of what are generally referred to in psychology as *expectancy effects*.

Maya mentions her interest in the Pygmalion experiment to the instructor, who suggests she read Rosenthal and Jacobson's book and look up a journal article by Stephen Raudenbush. The instructor does not recall exactly when or where the Raudenbush article was published but thinks it was in an APA journal in the 1980s. He tells Maya that Raudenbush published a frequently cited meta-analysis of all the Pygmalion experiments up to that time. The instructor advises Maya to use PsycINFO® to do an author search to find this article. He also suggests that she look up the terms *expectancy effect* and *Pygmalion experiment* in recent encyclopedias of psychology that the library has, and that she use PsycINFO again to do a more extensive search and retrieval after she has identified the *limited vocabulary* (also called the *control vocabulary*) that is appropriate to each electronic database. Using the appropriate vocabulary can prevent the frustration of searching with the "wrong" terms, but Maya decides to plunge forward on her own using the terms mentioned by her instructor.

Using the Online Catalog

Maya begins by finding her college library's Web page (which typically has a link on the university or college home page) and then finds the online catalog to search for the Rosenthal and Jacobson book. She types "Pygmalion in the classroom" in the search field, indicates that it is a "Title," and hits "Go." This gives her the book's call number, which tells her where to find this book in the library's stacks. Whether the book is currently in the library, checked out, or overdue is also indicated. For example, if *Pygmalion in the Classroom* has been checked out by someone a while ago and has still not been returned, Maya can ask the library to "recall" the book by asking the current user to return it.

Fortunately, this book is in the library, and Maya finds it and takes it to the circulation desk to check it out. While there, she asks about the location of encyclopedias of psychology, and the librarian points her to the location of several. She looks up *expectancy effects* in the indexes, reads the material, and finds that expectancy effects are also referred to as *experimenter expectancy effects*, and sometimes as *Rosenthal effects*, because Robert Rosenthal did landmark research on the topic. Maya takes notes, including jotting down relevant references and recommended readings that are cited in the encyclopedia articles; she may look into these sources later.

Some library Web sites may even have a floor plan that comes up when you click on the "Stacks" link, so you can mentally locate the book before going to the library. If Maya's library does not carry the Rosenthal and Jacobson book, she can order it through "interlibrary loan," as most libraries belong to groups of libraries that share materials and services. On the library's Web site, Maya will find such links as "Services," "Interlibrary loan," "Recall items," and "Request forms." If the book has been borrowed by someone, recalling it may take two or more weeks. Although it is convenient to use these links to order a book or to recall it, getting started early is clearly very important.

Using PsycINFO

To find the article by Stephen Raudenbush, Maya again uses the computer to access the library's reference databases. On the main page of the library's Web site, she finds PsycINFO listed under "Electronic databases" (or, in some libraries, "E-resources"). Many libraries list all the databases they subscribe to alphabetically, so you can scroll down to the one you are looking for. If the databases are organized by academic field (such as anthropology, marketing, psychology, etc.), then PsycINFO usually comes up first under psychology.

Maya clicks on PsycINFO and checks the place that says "Author"; she types in "Raudenbush" and clicks on the "Searches" button. A long list comes up of published works by this author, each item on the list linking to a PsycINFO record that also provides an abstract of the work. Maya scrolls down the list until she recognizes the article that her instructor mentioned and prints out the PsycINFO record (shown in Exhibit 4). Because the article is from an APA journal, there is a link in the online system to the article's full text in PsycARTICLES®. If the PsycINFO record had not been an APA journal, it is possible that the library would have a link to the full text in another database, especially if the journal is from one of the most well-known publishers. But even if there is no online full-text database, given the information in the PsycINFO record of the article (journal name, year, volume, and page numbers),[1] Maya knows how to track it down in the library. Having done all this, Maya has mastered about all the skills she will need to use any other electronic database to do a detailed search.

For now, Maya uses PsycINFO to begin her search of the literature in this database. The PsycINFO screen may vary from library to library, depending on the type of subscription the library has to this service. Maya begins by typing the book title but accidentally misspells it, typing "Pygmalian." Computers are both fussy and helpful; this search doesn't return any results, but the results screen does provide an alternate link under "Did you mean

---

[1]Sometimes an article is listed as "p. 6, 5pp," which means the article starts on page 6 and is 5 pages long, so you need to do the math to come up with the pages for the reference.

EXHIBIT 4 *PsycINFO record of journal article*

Accession Number	Peer Reviewed Journal: 1984-16218-001.
Title	Magnitude of teacher expectancy effects on pupil IQ as a function of the credibility of expectancy induction: A synthesis of findings from 18 experiments. [References].
Year of Publication	1984
Author	Raudenbush, Stephen W.
Source	Journal of Educational Psychology. Vol 76(1) Feb 1984, 85-97. American Psychological Assn.
Abstract	Meta-analysis was used to examine the variability in the outcomes of experiments testing the effects of teacher expectancy on pupil IQ. The tenuous process of expectancy induction, wherein researchers supply teachers with information designed to elevate their expectancies for children actually selected at random, is viewed as problematic in "Pygmalion" experiments, as developed by R. Rosenthal and L. Jacobson (1968). It was hypothesized that the better teachers know their pupils at the time of expectancy induction, the smaller the treatment effect would be. Data strongly support this hypothesis. Hypotheses that the type of IQ test (groups vs individual) and type of test administrator (aware vs blind to expectancy-inducing information) influence experimental results were not supported. The hypothesis that expectancy effects are larger for children in Grades 1 and 2 than for children in Grades 3-6 was supported. However, significant effects reappeared at Grade 7. Theoretical implications and questions for future meta-analytic research are discussed. (57 ref) (PsycINFO Database Record © 2006 APA, all rights reserved)

Source: Reprinted with permission of the American Psychological Association, publisher of the PsycINFO database © 2006.

'Pygmalion'?" Maya clicks it, and a dozen titles come up. For hypothesis ideas, she thinks this may be too small a number. But above the search field where she typed the title, she notices a check box to "Suggest subject terms." She checks it, and the search turns up more items, which she adds to her search string. She checks two of them and presses "Search," and this time, she gets several thousand results! To pare down, she clicks on "Peer reviewed journals" only, and the results are pared considerably. Now she tries a related subject selection ("Classroom environment") shown to the left of the results. A manageable number of items comes up.

Just the process of using the search engine has helped focus Maya's thoughts on the topic. She will try to come up with one or two hypotheses about the nature of the classroom environment and learning achievement. The search engine environment tends to immerse her in the topic and spurs her creativity in thinking about it. In the list, she can "Add" promising titles to an electronic folder. She selects titles regarding controlling classroom behavior, further narrowing her ideas for a hypothesis. When she opens the folder, she can delete, print, e-mail, save, or export the citations. She can also obtain a copy of most of the articles in the folder by clicking on a PDF link (a PDF file has a "picture" of each page, just as it appears in the original source). When she clicks to "Save" the list, she can even save the citations in APA format for the reference section of her paper. She copies and pastes the citations on the screen into a word-processing document for later retrieval into her paper (assuming she ends up citing them, of course). What a time-saver!

If this list of titles is insufficient for Maya's purposes, she can use the suggested subjects that PsycINFO provided to do more searches on the topic later. She makes a note of them and others that her instructor has mentioned for additional searches. She also notices that the browser has recorded her searches. She can, if desired, activate any one of them. This may be useful if she wants to try a different variation of an earlier search.

PsycARTICLES, PsycBOOKS, and PsycEXTRA

Maya used PsycINFO, the American Psychological Association's primary abstract database. The advantage of electronic databases like this one, as she discovered, is that you can search to your heart's content. Even if you do not have your own computer, the library usually has a bank of computers reserved for students. Because you may have to wait your turn to use one, ask whether there are computers in other locations that you can use to communicate with the automated system. If you have your own computer, you need to find out how to access these resources from your room. PsycINFO and other electronic databases each have their own limited vocabulary, which is appropriate to the particular database. For example, the print version of PsycINFO's limited vocabulary is the *Thesaurus of Psychological Index Terms* (published by the American Psychological Association), which is typically available in libraries that subscribe to PsycINFO.

There are many full-text databases, but few that are free online unless you are a student who can access them through your college library's Web site. The records in PsycINFO typically have a "journal link" that takes the user to the journal home page on the publisher's site, where you find out if the full text is free or not. (Some publishers put their journals up for free after an embargo period.) PsycARTICLES is the APA's full-text database for journals that go back to Volume 1, Issue 1. (The oldest APA journal, *Psychological Review,* goes back to 1894.) The APA also offers colleges and universities the opportunity to subscribe to another database called PsycBOOKS™, which lists books and a full-text record (PDF) of each chapter in the book for nearly all books published by APA, some historic books in the public domain, and 1,500 entries in the APA's *Encyclopedia of Psychology.* Another APA database, called PsycEXTRA, provides records and some full-text access to the "gray literature" (i.e., unpublished or hard-to-find work) that is not covered in PsycINFO and is outside the peer-review literature (conference papers, newspapers, technical reports, government reports, etc.).

Using InfoTrac® College Edition

Another full-text electronic database, InfoTrac College Edition, is packaged with this eighth edition of *Writing Papers*. To register on the log-in screen (http://www.infotrac-college.com), you enter a user name that you select and the password that came with your book (write down the user name and password for later use). After registering, you will find yourself at the keyboard search screen, where you type in search terms. You also specify the search strategy form you want InfoTrac College Edition to use; for example, indicating "In entire article content" will do a more extensive search for you than just indicating "In title, citation abstract." The browser also keeps a record of your searches under "History," so you can highlight one of your previous searches and press "View" to see the results of that particular search, useful if you want to try a different variation of an earlier search. Also an option is to check the box beside "To refereed publications," which means that only articles that have been reviewed by journal consultants (called *referees*) will be listed.

Once you have the list of refereed journal articles, you can set aside the titles you want to review by clicking in the box in front of each promising item. Then, using "View mark list" from the menu at the top, you can retrieve this marked subset. The retrieval options are under the marked list, at the bottom of the page. If you click the "Full article (if available)" option and also e-mail the article to yourself, you will receive a plain text version of each article, one e-mail per article. You also have the option to print the marked articles in plain text format, although you may prefer to save paper (and printing costs) by reading them first on screen on your computer. Next to the citations in your marked list, two icons (tiny pictures) may appear. One indicates that a plain text of the article is available (this is usually the case); the other icon looks like a little camera, indicating that graphics are included in the plain text. The graphics are shown in a reduced size in the text, but you can click on them to view them in full size.

As an illustration of the use of InfoTrac College Edition, Maya first tries "expectancy effects" and presses "Search," leaving all the other search choices unchanged. Fourteen items come up, most of them indirectly related to her interest. She goes back to the search page and tries "Pygmalion in the classroom" with the same settings. One long, full-text article appears, beneath which are links to articles on related topics, including newspaper articles. (It's always a good idea to scroll to the bottom of any Web page; there may be important stuff there.) On displaying these links, she can check any items and then "View mark list" from the menu at the top. If she chooses to "Print to browser," not only will she send to the printer, but the screen will show the citations formatted for copying and pasting (requiring just a little revision for proper APA style). She can also e-mail the list to herself in a form for automated importing by a bibliographic program.

Other tools are available on InfoTrac College Edition if you click on a link to an article. At the end of the plain text version that comes up, you can often use the Acrobat Reader (a special computer program) to see a PDF replica of the original article as it appeared in the journal. Most browsers have the Acrobat Reader already installed, but you can download it free at www.adobe.com. The PDF format is very convenient, but it can be time-consuming to download if you are using a dial-up connection. If you download articles in this format, save them to a disk or flash memory, because they will then be easier to read than the plain text version that is e-mailed or that appears with the link from the marked list. Additionally, at the end of each article is a menu of still more articles that are linked to related topics; this menu varies with each article. You may not need these articles now, but they may be useful when you research and write your paper later. This menu is yet another search feature branching out into the huge network of articles available on the Internet.

Tips on Using Other Electronic Databases

Once you are familiar with PsycINFO or InfoTrac College Edition, you should find it relatively easy to use other electronic databases to search for information. Exhibit 5 shows some of the many electronic databases that may be available to students through their library's Web page. Databases exist for just about every discipline and area of interest. Here are some tips for using these databases:

- Begin by writing down the questions you have, and then make a list of words or phrases you want to try as search terms.
- Scan the list of the databases that are available to you online; print the list if you can, to avoid having to remember them or endlessly going back and forth.
- Put a check mark next to any other databases that look relevant—or that might be of interest later on.
- As you search, keep a record so that you don't backtrack without realizing it; list the abstract or index, the years you searched, and the search terms that you used.
- If you can, copy what you find on a disk that you can look at again later. Before you open this file (or download it to your own hard drive), use your antivirus program to be sure that the file is not infected.
- Don't just make a citation list of relevant work; also read what you are going to cite because the instructor will wonder whether you have read it.

Notice at the bottom of Exhibit 5 a database called the Web of Science. If you need to do a more comprehensive search for a meta-analysis or a dissertation, the Web of Science will provide access to relatively recent records in the Social Sciences Citation Index (SSCI), Science Citation Index (SCI), and Arts & Humanities Citation Index (A&HCI). These databases are useful if you want to track down studies that followed up on an older study you've read about in your textbook. Once you are into the Web of Science, you can

EXHIBIT 5   Reference databases available electronically

Name	Coverage
Academic Search Premier	Full-text data from many scholarly publications in social science, the humanities, education, computer science, engineering, language and linguistics, arts and literature, medical science, and ethnic studies.
AskERIC	Bibliographic records of research reports, conference papers, teaching guides, books, and journal articles in education from preschool to the doctoral level; ERIC is an acronym for Educational Resources Information Center.
booksinprint.com	Full-text reviews of books in print, as well as out-of-print listings over the last decade.
britannica.com	Full-text database for *Encyclopedia Britannica* and *Merriam-Webster's Collegiate Dictionary.*
Census Lookup	Access to data tables for specific types of geographic areas from the most recent Census of Population and Housing; produced by the U.S. Census Bureau.
CQ Library	Full-text database for *CQ Weekly* and *CQ Researcher,* which provide legislative news about what is happening on Capitol Hill.
EDGAR	The Securities and Exchange Commission's database of electronic filings; acronym for the Electronic Data Gathering, Analysis, and Retrieval System.
Electronic Human Relations Area Files	Database of a nonprofit institution at Yale University, a consortium of educational, research, cultural, and government agencies in over 30 countries that provides ethnographic and related information by culture and subject; acronym is eHRAF.
GPO Access	U.S. Government Printing Office full-text documents and other informational links.
Harrison's Online	Full text of *Harrison's Principles of Internal Medicine,* a well-known medical textbook.
InfoTrac College Edition	Full-text database, packaged with *Writing Papers in Psychology;* provides access to the *Annual Review of Psychology* and many journals listed by discipline.
Internet Grateful Med	Health-related search information, including links to MEDLINE (national and international references to millions of articles in medicine, biomedicine, and related fields), AIDSLINE, HISTLINE (History of Medicine Online), and other Web sites.
JSTOR	Full text of back issues of periodicals across all disciplines.
LEXIS-NEXIS Academic UNIVerse	Full text of news reports, including business, medical, political, financial, and legal; a convenient source of news reports by topic areas.
MathSciNet	Research literature in mathematics, with emphasis on data in *Mathematical Reviews* and *Current Mathematical Publications.*

EXHIBIT 5   *Continued*

Name	Coverage
NCJRS Database	National Criminal Justice Reference Service database, including summaries of publications on criminal justice.
New Grove Dictionary	Full text of *The New Grove Dictionary of Music and Musicians* and *The New Grove Dictionary of Opera.*
OED Online	Full text of 20-volume *Oxford English Dictionary* and additions.
ProQuest Direct	Records of scholarly journals, periodicals, newspapers, and magazines in the University of Michigan archives, including charts, maps, photos, and some literature in full-text format.
PsycARTICLES	The American Psychological Association's full-text database of APA journal articles.
PsycBOOKS	The American Psychological Association's full-text database of chapters in books published by the APA, some historic books in the public domain, and the 1,500 entries in the APA's *Encyclopedia of Psychology.*
PsycCRITIQUES	The American Psychological Association's database of book and film reviews.
PsycEXTRA	The American Psychological Association's database of hard-to-find documents and records, such as conference papers and technical reports that exist outside of psychology's traditional peer-reviewed literature.
PsycINFO	The American Psychological Association's abstract database, including every abstract created by the APA back to 1887 in all areas of psychology.
Web of Science	Access to Social Sciences Citation Index (SSCI), the parent source of titles of works and names of authors, from 1989 to the present, as well as the Science Citation Index (also from 1989 forward).

click on the "Tutorial" button to get guidance, or you can click on the "Full search" (a general search) or the "Easy search" button (which allows a more limited search of articles on a specific topic, person, or address). This kind of search is called an *ancestry search* because you are tracking down "ancestral" citations of an older article or a book. For example, if you look up *Pygmalion in the Classroom,* you will get a long list of citations of this book.

Here are some more tips:

◆ Don't start out by using Google or Yahoo or MSN for your search and then rely on any documents that appear. Search engines like these generally seek what are called *statistic Web pages,* or thin, digitized layers of information that do not have search functions of their own. The electronic databases in Exhibit 5 are part of what is called the *deep Web,* which means they surface only when you make database queries from within the sites.

◆ However, Google does have a search engine, called Scholar, that might provide some sources you won't run across elsewhere. To get to Scholar, click on "More" on the Google home page, and select "Scholar." As is typical of Google searches, you'll get thousands of returns, but chances are good that the first few dozen will suit your purpose. (Maya typed in "classroom environment" and got over 500,000 hits.) The links may take you to other sites and require "Save/E-mail/Print" procedures that are different from (and usually not as convenient as) the procedures on PsycINFO or InfoTrac College Edition, but they are certainly worth a look. Each Google Scholar entry also includes the number of citations—a measure of how important and useful the work has been to others interested in the topic.

◆ As mentioned before, edifying Web sites are also linked to many textbooks; these Web sites are designed to help you make optimal use of the textbook and other course material. When you are using these Web sites, remember that you have a particular objective, so don't get distracted by tantalizing games (play with them after the semester is over).

And finally, if you are in a department that has many active researchers on the faculty, one of them may be working on the very problem that interests you. To find out, ask your instructor, and also ask if it will be OK to approach that person. If the answer is yes, set up an appointment to discuss your interests, but be sure to do your homework on the topic (and on the department's Web page) first. List for yourself the questions you want to ask, and then take notes during the interview.

Print Resources in the Library

A great many potentially relevant print resources are available in libraries, including dictionaries and other reference sources. For example, many libraries contain the print version of SSCI (Social Sciences Citation Index), which uses code letters to indicate the nature of the citation, such as *D* for "discussion" (conference item), *L* for letter," *M* for "meeting abstract," *N* for "technical note," *RP* for "reprint," or *W* for "computer review"; the absence of a code letter indicates an article, a report, a technical paper, or the like. There are also slang dictionaries that tell you the history of rhyming slang, African American slang, pig Latin, and so forth. If you are interested in the language used by the media, Richard Weiner is the author of *Webster's New World Dictionary of Media and Communications* (2nd ed., Macmillan, 1996) and a fascinating paperback book titled *The Skinny About Best Boys, Dollies, Green Rooms, Leads, and Other Media Lingo* (Random House, 2006). If you are interested in prominent people, you can look in *Current Biography* or *Who's Who*. If you want to know about famous Americans from the past, you can look in the *Dictionary of American Biography* or *Who Was Who in America*. The *Dictionary of National Biography* tells about men and women in British history. Librarians can point you to other works that you may find useful. Just remember that librarians are highly skilled in helping students find material. No matter how busy the librarian looks, you should not be intimidated. Don't be afraid to approach a librarian for help in finding resource material; that is the librarian's main purpose.

Another useful reference source, the *Annual Review of Psychology*, is available in full text on InfoTrac College Edition and is also available in print in many libraries. The *Annual Review of Psychology* is part of the *Annual Review* series, which is a serial publication (that is, one published at regular intervals) that provides reviews on just about every subject in science by leading authorities on specialized topics. Looking in the reference section of the *Annual Review of Psychology* can be a good way to find key studies. Other useful resources in psychology are called *handbooks;* if you search on this term in your library's online catalog, you are likely to find specialized handbooks. These edited books contain detailed reviews, and although the emphasis of handbook chapters is usually more idiosyncratic than the *Annual Review of Psychology* or the articles in encyclopedias, perusing several of these resources can help you formulate an overall picture of the particular area of research in which you are interested.

Some journals also specialize in integrative reviews. One of these is the highly respected *Psychological Bulletin* (a bimonthly publication of the APA). Another excellent one is *Perspectives on Psychological Science* (published by the Association for Psychological Science, or APS), and still another is the *Review of General Psychology* (a quarterly journal of the APA's Division of General Psychology). Two other highly respected journals, *Psychological Review* (another APA journal) and *Behavioral and Brain Sciences* (a quarterly published by Cambridge University Press), also publish integrative articles. One special feature of *Behavioral and Brain Sciences* is that, after each article, there is a section ("Open Peer Commentary") where you will find lively commentary on the article by other authors. The Association for Psychological Science, which has a Web site for students (http://www.psychologicalscience.org/apssc), publishes a supplement to its research journal (*Psychological Science*), called *Psychological Science in the Public Interest;* this is a semiannual monograph focusing on a single topic of public interest. Another useful APS journal is called *Current Directions in Psychology;* it publishes summary reviews of research findings. There are specialty journals in virtually any general area you can think of, and you can find out about them from your instructor.

Taking Notes in the Library

We have discussed retrieving abstracts and other material online and locating original material in the stacks, but not taking notes in the library. If you have the funds, the best way to make sure that your notes are exact is to photocopy the material you need. But be sure to write down in a conspicuous place on the photocopy the complete citation of all you copied. You will still need to interpret what you copied, and it is often easier to make notes of your interpretation at the time you first have the material in hand. Having such notes will enable you to write an accurate paper as well as one that is efficiently organized. You can write your interpretations on the back of your photocopies so that your notes are handy when it is time to organize all your work.

Making detailed notes will also help you avoid committing *plagiarism* accidentally. We will have more to say about this problem later in this book, but you plagiarize intentionally when you knowingly copy or summarize someone's work without acknowledging the source, or when you put your name on a paper that someone else wrote. You plagiarize accidentally when you copy someone's work but forget to credit it or to put it in quotation marks. Plagiarism is illegal, and you should guard against it by keeping accurate notes, giving credit to others when it is due, and not claiming someone else's work as your own.

If you are taking extensive notes on a laptop computer, you need some way to distance yourself from pages and pages of notes in order to bring coherence to them. The same is true if you are taking handwritten notes in the library. Some writers like to use a separate index card for each idea that they find as they uncover relevant material. Some prefer making notes on 5 × 8-inch index cards because they can usually get all the information they want on the front of a large card, so it is easier to find what they want later. If you are using a computer to take notes, you can print them out and cluster them in logical batches (as you would large index cards). For each note, be sure to include the full reference of the material, including all the information you will need for the reference section of your paper, as well as the page numbers of verbatim quotes (to cite in the narrative of your paper).

If you have made an outline for a literature review (as described in chapter 5), you can code each card or printout with the particular outline section where the material will be used (or you can use color coding). An alternative is to use a folder for each section of your literature review, and then to file the relevant batches in the appropriate folder. In this way, you can maintain a general organization of your notes and avoid facing a huge stack of miscellaneous bits and pieces of information that you must sort and integrate into a useful order. If you are using reference numbers to code material, be consistent, because a haphazard arrangement will only slow you down when it is time to write the first draft.

The most fundamental rule of note taking is to be thorough and systematic so that you do not waste time and energy having to return to the same book or article. Because memory is porous, it is better to photocopy or record too much than to rely on recall to fill in the gaps. Be sure your notes will make sense to you when you examine them later.

Source Credibility

Not all information is reliable, and the question is how to separate the credible from the suspect. This question is not easy to answer: A source of information that one person views as credible may not be perceived by another the same way. The way to address this problem is to subject manuscripts submitted to respected journals to *peer review* (that is, the editors send them out to experts in the same field for independent evaluations and recommendations). It is certainly not impossible for a poorly done study to slip by occasionally, but as a general rule, researchers give greater weight to peer-reviewed journal articles than to unpublished manuscripts, technical reports, or chapters in edited books (which may be lightly reviewed, if at all). Textbooks are sent out for review, but mostly because the prospective publisher wants to find out whether they will be saleable.

Even within the peer-reviewed literature, there is a pecking order of journals in any field. Manuscripts that are rejected by one journal may be sent to a second or third journal, until they finally find homes. Articles in journals at the top of the pecking order are not automatically more credible than those in other journals, but a social hierarchy of journals does exist in every field, and the toughest journals in which to publish are usually those at the top of the social structure. In some cases, 85% or more of manuscripts submitted to the most prestigious journals are rejected by the editors based on peer reviews, but some manuscripts may be returned without review because, in the editor's judgment, they seem to be inappropriate for that particular journal. Robert J. Sternberg, a widely published psychologist, wisely cautioned that "the place of publication is not a valid proxy for the quality and impact of the research" (*APA Observer,* October 2001, p. 40).

Some information is especially suspect, however, such as that in chat rooms on the Web. There is, in fact, a growing literature in psychological science on the nature of these chat rooms and the fertile ground they provide for rumors to take root. Because in a given instance it might be hard to decide whether something you read online is a fact or a rumor (i.e., an unsupported allegation) or maybe even a boldfaced lie, the saying about "buying a pig in a poke" is applicable to much of this information. The best guidance we can give you is this: When in doubt, ask your instructor for guidance.

Additional Tips When Starting Your Literature Search

As you get started on the literature search, try to be realistic in assessing how much material you will need in your review. Too few journal articles or books may result in a weak foundation for your project, but too much material and intemperate expectations may overwhelm you and your topic. You are writing not a doctoral dissertation or an article for a journal but a required paper that must be completed within a limited amount of time. How can you find out what is a happy medium between too little and too much? Talk with your instructor before you start an intensive literature search. Ask whether your plan seems realistic.

Here are some more tips to get you started on the literature search and retrieval and to do it efficiently:

◆ Ask the instructor to recommend any key works that you should read or consult. Even if you feel confident about your topic already, asking the instructor for specific leads can prevent your going off on a tangent.

◆ Do not expect to finish your literature search and retrieval in one sitting. Students with unrealistic expectations make themselves overly anxious and rush a task that should be done patiently and methodically to achieve the best result.

◆ Suppose you cannot locate the original work that you are looking for in the stacks. Some students return repeatedly to the library, day after day, seeking a book or journal article before discovering that it has been lost or stolen or is being rebound. Ask a librarian to find the elusive material. If the original work you need is unavailable, the librarian may consult another college library. However, the material could take so long to arrive that you might miss the deadline set by your instructor (this kind of delay is not an acceptable excuse).

◆ If you are looking for a specialized work, you probably will not find it in a small public library, so don't waste your time. When students spend a lot of time off campus in public libraries and bookstores looking for source material, they usually come back with references from general texts or current mass-market books and periodicals, and these rarely constitute acceptable sources.

◆ Remember to keep a running checklist of the sources you searched and the search terms you used so that you don't accidentally retrace your steps.

Library and E-mail Etiquette

Before we turn to the basics of developing your proposal for a review paper or a research project, here is some final advice about using the library. The golden rule of library etiquette is to respect your library and remember that others also have to use it:

◆ Be quiet.
◆ Never tear pages out of journals or books.
◆ Never write in library journals or books.
◆ Do not monopolize material or machines.
◆ Return books and periodicals as soon as you finish with them.

Many students are surprised to learn that they can communicate with busy researchers. There is no guarantee that you will get a reply, but if you do make a request by e-mail, here are some dos and don'ts of e-mail etiquette:

◆ Don't ask for something readily available in most college libraries, because it is going to sound as if you were too lazy to look for it.

◆ Do indicate in the subject space the nature of your e-mail message (for example, "Reprint request"), or else it may be deleted as spam without ever being opened.

◆ Don't write an overly detailed message; say who you are and what you are "requesting" (the polite way of asking), and thank the person in advance.

◆ Don't expect a lengthy response.

◆ If you are requesting a reprint, it is likely to be transmitted as a PDF or Word file, so do make sure that your computer can open both of these kinds of files.

◆ If you receive a response, do thank the person.

3

Developing a Proposal

Once you have chosen your topic, retrieved background
information, and crystallized your ideas, the next step is
to develop a proposal. Some instructors feel that an oral
presentation is sufficient, but most require a written proposal
as a way of ensuring that both they and their students have
a common understanding of the topic, the importance of
originality in each student's work, and a clear sense of all
ethical issues in proposed research studies.

Object of the Proposal

The object of your proposal is to tell the instructor what you would like to
study. However, it is not a one-way communication, but an opportunity for
the instructor to provide feedback and to raise questions that you need to
address before going any further. If your assignment is an empirical research
study, the proposal is also an opportunity to anticipate and address ethical
concerns that might be raised. You might think of the research proposal as
a kind of "letter of agreement" between you and the instructor. Once the
research proposal has been approved, it is presumed that you will consult
with the instructor before making changes in any aspect of the procedure. A
proposal for a literature review usually has more room for flexibility. It gives
the instructor an opportunity to see whether you may be embarking on too
grand a literature review in the limited time available. It would be unreason-
able to expect you to know already what you will conclude, although you
probably have preliminary ideas that you can express about the direction of
your review.

Instructors may require submissions in addition to a written proposal,
and they may ask for details besides those in the sample proposals in this

chapter. In these sample proposals, the students are responding to the instructors' questions about how the idea for the project originated and why the topic is worth studying. The purpose of such questions is (a) to stimulate you to formulate plans, (b) to encourage you to choose a topic you find intrinsically interesting, and (c) to make sure that these are your ideas. We will have more to say about the third point later in this book, but it is absolutely essential that the work be your own even if it builds on, or is a replication of, previous work by others.

In fact, replication is regarded as an essential criterion of credible scientific knowledge because it continues the discovery process of science as it clarifies and expands the meanings and limits of theories, hypotheses, and observations. Someone once compared the scientist to a person trying to unlock a door using a hitherto untried key. The role of replication, we might say, is to make the "key" available to others so they can see for themselves whether or not it works in a particular situation, and also how many other doors it can open. Replicating a published study does not mean merely reproducing a similar p value, however, because the p value is sensitive to the number of sampling units (for example, the total number of research subjects), the magnitude of the effect, the variability of scores, and so forth. We will have more to say about p values in chapter 6, but replicating a study means observing a similar relationship or phenomenon. Suppose you are out jogging and spotted two Martians—not two people disguised as Martians for Halloween, but *real* Martians: you know, green skin, antennas poking out of their scalps, and all the rest. You are not going to boot up your computer or whip out your calculator to run a significance test, but you sure are going to ask the nearest earthling, "Do you see what I see?"

Replications are sometimes the basis of senior theses and course projects. However, the student is expected to add a creative touch to the design, usually in the form of a new hypothesis or some other innovative aspect. For example, if the study you are replicating used two levels of the independent variable, you might experiment with three or four levels to find out whether there is a linear or a nonlinear relationship between the independent and dependent variables. If you can think of a variable that might alter the relationship between the independent and dependent variables (that is, a moderator variable), then you can design a replication around your hypothesis of a moderator variable. Or you might choose a different measure of the dependent variable to see whether the original results are generalizable to more than one measure. Of course, you will want to design your study so that it is similar to the original study even while you are studying your own innovative idea; otherwise, you will find yourself in a logical bind if you need to explain any discrepancies between your results and the earlier study's. If you are writing a proposal for a replication study, it is a good idea to tell how you plan to compare the results. Do you propose a quantitative comparison of effect sizes (using a simple meta-analytic procedure) or a qualitative analysis based on theoretically relevant characteristics, or perhaps a combination of both?

The Literature Review Proposal

Exhibit 6 illustrates one form of the kind of information that might be reported in a proposal for a literature review. Although your instructor may ask you for other information or require a different format, this exhibit will at least get you thinking about what typically belongs in a proposal for a review paper. As one instructor wrote to us about what she told students, the proposal should show your understanding that your writing assignment must present a reasoned and organized argument that leads somewhere, not just an unfocused hodgepodge of literature that falls under the same keyword. It is also important to show that the final paper will consist of *your* ideas, because college instructors are especially attuned to the issue of originality in student writing assignments.

It is clear that John Smith's ideas did not come out of the blue, and that he met with the instructor even before drafting this proposal in order to get preliminary feedback. He got his initial idea from the instructor's lecture and soon afterward began to look up relevant references. He has an impressive preliminary list of references, but he states that he plans to use PsycINFO ("and possibly other electronic databases") to search for relevant articles. He realizes that a lot has been written about the two theoretical orientations he proposes to review, so he wisely cautions that, because of time constraints, he will be able to read only a fraction of the literature on this topic. That John and the instructor have mutual interests in Gardner's theory of multiple intelligences (because she has done research on it) will be a boon to John as he begins to think about pulling ideas together, and he mentions that he plans to sign up periodically to meet with the instructor.

Regarding the format of the proposal, notice that John's name is typed above each page beside the page number; typing his name at the top of each page serves as a safety device if any pages get accidentally detached. Some instructors prefer that students insert a *page header* (a couple of words from the title), like the page headers in the final review paper in appendix B. John gives his e-mail address or other contact information, making it easy for the instructor to communicate with him. John summarizes the *focus* of his proposed review as he envisions it right now, knowing that it may change a little as he gets deeper into the project. He next describes the *background and objective,* emphasizing the originality of his idea and his tentative plan for pulling the literature together. John's description of his *literature search strategy* is evidence that he is not floundering and, instead, has a clear direction for his search and retrieval. The proposal ends with a preliminary list of references formatted in APA style. John's proposal is written in a way indicating that he has put a lot of effort and thought into this assignment.

EXHIBIT 6   *Sample proposal for a literature review*

John Smith 1

Proposal for a Literature Review

John Smith (e-mail address or other contact information)

(Date the proposal is submitted)

Focus of the Review

    To examine two theoretical orientations regarding the nature of human intelligence, the traditional g-centered view versus the more recent assumption of multiple intelligences.

Background and Objective

    The idea for this project came out of the instructor's lecture on intelligence testing. She spoke of the work of Howard Gardner and his theory of multiple intelligences. She also described her own research on a facet of Gardner's work, which he called *interpersonal intelligence*. I found some of Gardner's books in the college library (Gardner, 1983, 1991, 1993a, 1993b, 1999) and have been reading them and taking notes. I understand that this work is part of a movement away from the traditional view of IQ that has predominated in psychology and education for many years (cf. Ceci & Liker, 1986; Riggio & Pirozzolo, 2002; Sternberg & Detterman, 1986; Sternberg & Wagner, 1986).

    According to the traditional view, there is a general factor (called the g factor) that is common to all standard measures of intelligence and IQ (Spearman, 1927). The more recent approach of Gardner and others (e.g., Ceci, 1990, 1996; Ceci & Liker, 1986; Sternberg, 1985, 1988, 1990) emphasizes the idea of several distinctive types of intelligence, such as (in Gardner's research) logical-mathematical intelligence, linguistic intelligence, spatial intelligence, and interpersonal and intrapersonal intelligence. The objective of this literature review is to examine the traditional g-centered IQ orientation and the multiple-intelligences approach, including how they originated, how they differ, and what is the rationale for each. Since each has its strong proponents and critics, I am also interested in looking at the areas of controversy and disagreement.

EXHIBIT 6   Continued

John Smith 2

Literature Search Strategy

The textbook in this course has a long discussion of intelligence (Kaplan & Saccuzzo, 2005), and as noted above, I have begun reading and taking notes from the work of Gardner (1983, 1993a, 1993b), Sternberg (1985, 1990), and Ceci (1996). From reading an article by Gilbert (1971) in *The Encyclopedia of Education,* I know that the concept of intelligence has been awash in controversy for years. The instructor suggested that I consult another popular textbook on psychological testing (Anastasi & Urbina, 1997) to get another perspective on this subject. I also plan to use PsycINFO (and possibly other electronic databases) to search for relevant articles.

Because of time constraints, I can expect to read only a fraction of the vast literature on intelligence (there is a journal called *Intelligence* as well as an encyclopedia devoted to this subject, the *Encyclopedia of Human Intelligence*). I plan to sign up periodically to meet with the instructor to discuss the progress of this review and my tentative ideas. I have taken a psychological statistics course, and I think I should be able to make sense of any basic quantitative information in the material I read, but I will certainly ask for help if I run into a problem.

On the following pages are the relevant books and articles that I have found so far. Any suggestions for additional material will be appreciated, though I expect that I will only be able to skim some of these works because of the press of other course requirements.

EXHIBIT 6 *Continued*

John Smith 3

References

Anastasi, A., & Urbina, S. (1997). *Psychological testing* (7th ed.). Upper Saddle River, NJ: Prentice Hall.

Ceci, S. J. (1990). *On intelligence . . . more or less: A bioecological treatise on intellectual development.* Englewood Cliffs, NJ: Prentice Hall.

Ceci, S. J. (1996). *On intelligence: A bioecological treatise on intellectual development* (Expanded ed.). Cambridge, MA: Harvard University Press.

Ceci, S. J., & Liker, J. (1986). Academic and nonacademic intelligence: An experimental separation. In R. J. Sternberg & R. Wagner (Eds.), *Practical intelligence: Origins of competence in the everyday world* (pp. 119–142). New York: Cambridge University Press.

Gardner, H. (1983). *Frames of mind: The theory of multiple intelligences.* New York: Basic Books.

Gardner, H. (1991). *The unschooled mind: How children think and how schools should teach.* New York: Basic Books.

Gardner, H. (1993a). *Creating minds: An anatomy of creativity seen through the lives of Freud, Einstein, Picasso, Stravinsky, Eliot, Graham, and Ghandi.* New York: Basic Books.

Gardner, H. (1993b). *Multiple intelligences: The theory in practice.* New York: Basic Books.

Gardner, H. (1999). *Intelligence reframed: Multiple intelligences for the 21st century.* New York: Basic Books.

Gilbert, H. B. (1971). Intelligence tests. In L. C. Deighton (Ed.), *The encyclopedia of education* (Vol. 5, pp. 128–135). New York: Macmillan & Free Press.

Guilford, J. P. (1967). *The nature of intelligence.* New York: McGraw-Hill.

Herrnstein, R. J., & Murray, C. (1994). *The bell curve: Intelligence and class structure in American life.* New York: Free Press.

Kaplan, R. M., & Saccuzzo, D. P. (2005). *Psychological testing: Principles, applications, and issues* (6th ed.). Belmont, CA: Thomson Wadsworth.

EXHIBIT 6 *Continued*

John Smith 4

Neisser, U., Boodoo, G., Bouchard, T. J., Jr., Boykin, A. W., Brody, N., Ceci, S. J., et al. (1996). Intelligence: Knowns and unknowns. *American Psychologist, 51,* 77–101.

Riggio, R. E., Murphy, S. E., & Pirozzolo, F. J. (Eds.). (2002). *Multiple intelligences and leadership.* Mahwah, NJ: Erlbaum.

Rosnow, R. L., Skleder, A. A., Jaeger, M. E., & Rind, B. (1994). Intelligence and the epistemics of interpersonal acumen: Testing some implications of Gardner's theory. *Intelligence, 19,* 93–116.

Spearman, C. (1927). *The abilities of man.* New York: Macmillan.

Sternberg, R. J. (Ed.). (1982). *Handbook of human intelligence.* New York: Cambridge University Press.

Sternberg, R. J. (1985). *Beyond IQ: A triarchic theory of human intelligence.* New York: Cambridge University Press.

Sternberg, R. J. (1988). *The triarchic mind: A new theory of human intelligence.* New York: Viking.

Sternberg, R. J. (1990). *Metaphors of mind: A new theory of human intelligence.* New York: Cambridge University Press.

Sternberg, R. J., & Detterman, D. K. (Eds.). (1986). *What is intelligence? Contemporary viewpoints on its nature and definition.* Norwood, NJ: Ablex.

Sternberg, R. J., & Wagner, R. (Eds.). (1986). *Practical intelligence: Nature and origins of competence in the everyday world.* New York: Cambridge University Press.

Thurstone, L. L., & Thurstone, T. G. (1941). *Factorial studies of intelligence.* Chicago: University of Chicago Press.

Vandenberg, S. G. (1971). Genetics of intelligence. In L. C. Deighton (Ed.), *The encyclopedia of education* (Vol. 5, pp. 117–128). New York: Macmillan & Free Press.

The Research Proposal

Exhibit 7 illustrates one form of a proposal for a research project. Jane Doe begins by telling how she came up with her idea and also what preliminary work she has done. Particularly impressive is that after getting the instructor's tentative OK, she contacted a restaurant where she could run the study. She has already informed the restaurant owner and the server about the nature of her proposed research and gotten their written approval to show to the instructor. Once her proposal has been approved, Jane will be able to get started. Her three experimental hypotheses are well reasoned and precisely stated, another indication that she has already done a lot of preliminary work. The more thorough Jane is, the more focused the instructor's comments can be as he continues to shepherd Jane toward her goal. If you plan to develop a questionnaire or an interview schedule, put a preliminary verbal sketch of it in the proposal so the instructor can give you feedback with specific suggestions.

Jane's *proposed method* is also precise. She tells why she has settled on a total N of 80 dining parties. She also describes exactly how the four conditions will be randomly chosen by the waitress and what the particular procedure will be in each condition. In discussing the *scoring and analysis* of the findings, she begins by telling how the dependent variable will be operationalized. She gives credit to the instructor for suggesting how to deal with nonsignificant results due to underpowered tests. In describing her plan for computing a contrast to test the overall prediction, Jane believes that the data analysis is not beyond her statistical ability. If there is a problem, this student is not someone who will be shy about asking for further guidance, as she is clearly diligent, motivated, energetic, and goal-directed. There is a brief discussion of *ethical considerations*, although some instructors may require that a standard form be completed, signed by the student, and attached to the proposal. Jane's proposal concludes with a list of the studies that she has cited. The level of detail in this proposal reflects the considerable amount of time that she has spent arriving at this stage and her consultations with the instructor on more than one occasion.

Ethical Considerations

As noted above, Jane Doe's discussion of ethics is brief, but other proposals may call for a more detailed discussion or a standard form that needs to be filled out, signed, and submitted. The student may also be asked to provide a stronger rationale or to provide other relevant information. The reason that instructors require a detailed discussion is that ethical accountability is an important consideration in every aspect of research. The absolute requirements of ethical accountability are (a) that you, the researcher, will protect the dignity, privacy, and safety of your subjects; (b) that your study will be technically sound (so as not to waste precious resources, including the subjects' time and effort); and (c) that the research will not be detrimental to society.

EXHIBIT 7   *Sample proposal for a research project*

Jane Doe 1

Proposal for a Research Project

Jane Doe (e-mail address or other contact information)

(Date the proposal is submitted)

Focus of the Research

  To conduct a randomized, naturalistic experiment in a restaurant, in which I propose to investigate the relative extent to which several simple techniques for offering diners after-meal candies may affect the percentage amounts they tip the server.

Background and Hypotheses

  This summer I have a job as a waitress in a restaurant in Ogunquit, Maine. When the instructor told about the naturalistic experiments he had done on tipping behavior (Rind & Bordia, 1995, 1996), he got me thinking that this topic might be suitable for my research project. The instructor directed me to an article by Lynn (1996) and other work on restaurant tipping by Garrity and Degelman (1990), Hornik (1992), Lynn and Mynier (1993), and Tidd and Lockard (1978). In a social psychology course last semester, we learned about reciprocity theory, and that theory also seems relevant to the research that I am proposing. I plan to do a further literature search using PsycINFO, though I believe I now have enough background information to justify three experimental predictions.

  Research findings in the articles cited above are consistent with the idea that servers who are seen as friendly are likely to receive larger tips. For example, techniques such as a friendly touch or a smiling face drawn on the check have been found to increase the resulting tip percentage. The proposed research is in this vein, in that another simple technique for fostering an impression of server friendliness may be to have the server personally offer each diner an after-meal treat of a complimentary chocolate candy. There will be a control (no candy) condition and three experimental conditions (as described below) based on the interaction between the server and the diners when the check is presented.

EXHIBIT 7   Continued

Jane Doe 2

Three experimental hypotheses will be tested. First, the mere offer of a candy (called the *1-piece condition*) will have the effect of increasing tips, compared with the *no-candy control.* Second, assuming this effect is cumulative, offering diners two candies (called the *2-piece condition*) will increase tipping still more in comparison with the control. Third, as people often feel obligated to return a favor (Regan, 1971), creating the impression that offering a second piece of candy reflects a generous impulse on the part of the server will elicit even larger tips (called the *1 + 1 condition*). Thus, I predict that tips will increase from the control to the 1-piece to the 2-piece to the 1 + 1 condition.

Proposed Method

Participants. After discussing the proposed research with the instructor in a preliminary way, and getting his approval to proceed to the next stage, I asked an acquaintance who owns a restaurant whether I could have permission to conduct the study there. Attached to this proposal is the written permission of the restaurant owner and also the permission of a female server who has agreed to participate. They have also agreed to let me randomly assign 80 dining parties to the four conditions. Based on a power analysis using a table in the course text, the statistical power of three *t* tests of simple effects would be approximately .80 (which was the recommended level), assuming an effect size of approximately $r = .5$.

Procedure. The conditions (control, 1-piece, 2-piece, 1 + 1) will be written on 80 index cards, so each card describes one of the four conditions. The cards will be shuffled and given to the server, who will select a card blindly from her apron pocket just before presenting the check. The server will also be given a basket containing an assortment of wrapped miniature chocolates. In the *control condition,* the server will present the check, thank the dining party, and immediately leave the table in order to avoid any nonessential interaction. In the remaining three conditions, the server will bring along the basket of candy. In the *1-piece condition,* the server will offer each person in the dining party one candy of his or her choice, will thank the diners after their selection, and will leave the table. In the *2-piece condition,* the server will offer each person two

EXHIBIT 7 Continued

candies, thank the diners after their selections, and leave. In the *1 + 1 condition,* the
server will offer each person a candy and then say, "Oh, have another piece," in order to
create the impression that the treat is a generous afterthought; the server will then thank
the diners and leave the table. After the party has left the restaurant, the server will
record on the same index card that was used to specify the condition (a) the amount of
the tip, (b) the amount of the bill before taxes, and (c) the size of the dining party.

Scoring and Analysis

The dependent measure will be the tip percentage, the amount of the tip divided by
the amount of the bill before taxes, then multiplied by 100. The basic results will be
reported in the form of means, 95% confidence intervals around the means, and standard
deviations. Three independent-sample *t* tests will be used to compare each of the three
treatment conditions (1-piece, 2-piece, and 1 + 1) with the control condition, and effect
sizes and their 95% confidence intervals will be reported.

When I met with the instructor, he raised the possibility that the observed effects
may not be as large as $r = .5$, in which case I will not have the benefit of working with
power of .8. Although there is not much I can do about increasing the total N (because
of time constraints and the agreement with the owner of the restaurant and the server),
the instructor suggested I think of the *t* tests as a posteriori tests after an overall
ANOVA. This option would justify using the pooled S^2 and its associated degrees of
freedom ($df = N - k = 80 - 4 = 76$) for each *t* test. For the effect size correlations
computed from these *t* tests, the *df* would still be defined by the groups being compared
($df = n_1 + n_2 - 2 = 20 + 20 - 2 = 38$), as described in the course text.

The instructor also recommended that I compute a 1×4 contrast F(or t) to test
the prediction that the tip percentage will increase from the control to the 1-piece to the
2-piece to the 1 + 1 condition (using contrast weights of −3, −1, +1, +3, respectively). I
realize that also reporting an overall ANOVA will not address my specific predictions,
but the ANOVA summary table would be a way to show how the contrast F can be
carved out of the overall between-groups sum of squares. I can do the overall ANOVA

EXHIBIT 7 *Continued*

Jane Doe 4

using the statistics program we have been taught, and it would be a convenient way to obtain the pooled S^2 (i.e., the MS_{within}).

Ethical Considerations

The study involves a mild deception in that the diners will be unaware that they are participating in an experiment. I do not propose to debrief them because no potential risk is involved. I cannot ask people who are dining whether they agree to "participate in an experiment," because that would destroy the credibility of the manipulation and render the results scientifically meaningless. I have also agreed to give the owner and the server full details of the results, and not to mention their names or the name of the restaurant in any research reports. All tips will be the property of the server.

EXHIBIT 7 *Continued*

Jane Doe 5

References

Garrity, K., & Degelman, D. (1990). Effect of server introduction on restaurant tipping. *Journal of Applied Social Psychology, 20,* 168–172.

Hornik, J. (1992). Tactile stimulation and consumer response. *Journal of Consumer Research, 19,* 449–458.

Lynn, M. (1996). Seven ways to increase servers' tips. *Cornell Hotel and Restaurant Administration Quarterly, 37*(3), 24–29.

Lynn, M., & Mynier, K. (1993). Effect of server posture on restaurant tipping. *Journal of Applied Social Psychology, 23,* 678–685.

Regan, D. T. (1971). Effects of a favor and liking on compliance. *Journal of Experimental Social Psychology, 7,* 627–639.

Rind, B., & Bordia, P. (1995). Effect of server's "thank you" and personalization on restaurant tipping. *Journal of Applied Social Psychology, 25,* 745–751.

Rind, B., & Bordia, P. (1996). Effect on restaurant tipping of male and female servers drawing a happy, smiling face on the backs of customers' checks. *Journal of Applied Social Psychology, 26,* 218–225.

Tidd, K., & Lockard, J. (1978). Monetary significance of the affiliative smile: A case for reciprocal altruism. *Bulletin of the Psychometric Society, 11,* 344–346.

Here are some specific questions to get you thinking about the ethics of your proposed study:

◆ Might there be any psychological or physical risks to the research participants? How do you plan to avoid these risks?

◆ Will any deception be used, and if so, is it really necessary, or can you think of a way to avoid using deception?

◆ How do you plan to debrief the subjects? If you really must use a deception, then how will you "dehoax" the deceived subjects? How can you be sure that the dehoaxing procedure has been effective?

◆ If you are planning to use volunteer subjects, how do you plan to recruit them, and can you be sure that the recruitment procedure is noncoercive?

◆ How do you plan to use informed consent and to ensure that the participants understand they are free to withdraw at any time without penalty?

◆ What steps will you take to ensure the confidentiality of the data?

Tempus Fugit

Because time flies when you are writing an assigned paper, here are two final tips:

1. *Turn in your proposal on time.* Instructors are also very busy people, and they (like you) schedule their work. Turning in a proposal late is like waving a red flag that signals the wrong message to your instructor. Instead of communicating that you are responsible and reliable and someone who thinks clearly, this red flag signals that you may be none of the above.

2. *Be precise.* In Lewis Carroll's *Through the Looking Glass*, Alice (of *Alice in Wonderland*) comes upon Humpty Dumpty, who uses a word in a way that Alice says she does not understand. He smiles contemptuously and says, "Of course you don't—till I tell you. . . . When *I* use a word, it means just what I choose it to mean—neither more nor less." Unlike Humpty Dumpty, you do not have the luxury of telling your instructor to "take it or leave it." Nor do you have the extra time to keep resubmitting the proposal because you did not make the initial effort to be precise.

4

Planning the Research Report

The basic structure and form of research reports in psychology have evolved over many years. In this chapter, we describe this structure in the context of the sample report in appendix A. Familiarity with these matters will enable you to organize your thoughts and plan the first draft (discussed in chapter 7). (If you are writing a review paper, you can skip this chapter and go on to chapter 5.)

Three Broad Types of Research

Research methods texts routinely cover data collection and data analysis, and we will assume that you are mastering those techniques (though we have more to say about reporting statistical information in chapter 6). What primarily remains is developing a final report that will explain in clear language (a) what you did, (b) why you did it, (c) what you found out, (d) what your findings mean, and (e) what you have concluded. Research methods texts usually make fine distinctions among the various kinds of research strategies, such as the laboratory experiment, the sample survey, the case study, and the archival approach. The study reported by Jane Doe in appendix A illustrates another strategy, a randomized experiment in a naturalistic setting. Over and above these differences is another distinction among three broad types of research orientations, referred to as *descriptive, relational* (also called *correlational*), and *experimental*. Each orientation has its own objective, reflected in the answers given to the five questions mentioned above.

The usual purpose of descriptive research in human psychology is to map out an aspect of how people feel, think, or behave. The researcher might raise theoretical ideas or discuss ideas for further research, but the primary focus of the research report will be describing as carefully as possible what was observed and measured. In other words, the object of this type of research orientation is to describe how things are. Sooner or later, however, someone will want to know *how* what happens behaviorally is related to other variables. The "how" is the object of the relational research orientation, which is an examination of how certain variables are related or how the behavior of interest is correlated with certain events. The researcher would indicate not just whether two variables are significantly related (the *p* level), but also the form of the relationship (e.g., linear or nonlinear, positive or negative) and the effect size (the magnitude of the observed relationship). The third broad type, the experimental orientation, is focused more on the identification of determining factors, or causes (i.e., how things get to be the way they are, or what leads to what). Relational research can only rarely provide such insights, and then only under special conditions. We will have more to say about the language of "causality" in a later chapter, but it is especially important when reporting a descriptive or relational study not to use language that implies that changes in one variable are *responsible* for changes in another.

Suppose that in a cognitive psychology or developmental psychology course the instructor mentions a review article by Paul Bloom and Deena Skolnick Weisberg, published in *Science* magazine (2007, vol. 316, pp. 996–997). The authors summarized a wide variety of descriptive, relational, and experimental findings that are relevant to the question of how and why children and adults sometimes resist scientific information that clashes with their commonsense intuitions. A descriptive study might call for the mapping out of first graders' commonsense beliefs and assumptions. A relational (or correlational) study might explore the relationship between those beliefs or assumptions and specific demographic factors. An experimental study might investigate whether the teacher's presenting the children with scientific facts results in a greater acceptance of those facts than, say, if they were presented by someone dressed as SpongeBob SquarePants.

Here is another example: Suppose a student is interested in the psychology of rumor and gossip as a possible topic for empirical research, but he needs to narrow his interest. The student might begin by looking up these terms in the *APA Dictionary of Psychology:*

> **gossip 1.** *n.* idle personal talk or communication often unsubstantiated information. Gossip may be scandalous in content or malicious in intention. **2.** *vb.* To engage in such talk.
> **rumor** *n.* a story or piece of information of unknown reliability that is passed from person to person. See also GOSSIP.

Both phenomena seem pretty amorphous, but rumor seems less vague and may not be such an elusive concept to study. Using PsycINFO, the student finds a recent book on rumor by Nicholas DiFonzo and Prashant Bordia, titled *Rumor Psychology: Social and Organizational Approaches* (American Psychological Association, 2007). The authors discussed the results of many descriptive, relational, and experimental studies of rumor. Inspired by that discussion, for a descriptive study the student might collect and then sort rumors into different categories. For a relational study, the student might investigate plausible correlates of whether rumors that forecast pleasant events are passed with greater or less frequency than rumors that forecast unpleasant events. For an experimental study, the student might randomly administer different experimental treatments in order to manipulate certain conditions theorized to affect rumor generation and transmission.

The Basic Structure

Whether a report describes descriptive, relational, or experimental research, a well-written paper implies a logical progression in thought. By adhering to the structure described in the remainder of this chapter, you can create this kind of order in your finished paper. In chapter 1, we noted that instructors generally expect research reports to typically include (a) an abstract, (b) an introduction, (c) a method section, (d) a results section, (e) a discussion of the results, and (f) a list of the references cited. Observe, however, in Jane Doe's research report (in appendix A) that there are more parts in her manuscript than these six. Although you may not need all of them in your research report (or, alternatively, you may want to report some results in a figure rather than, or in addition to, a table), Jane's research report contains the following parts:

Title page
Abstract
Introduction
Method
Results
Discussion
References
Appendix
Author note
Footnotes
Tables

Except for the layout of the title page and the addition of an appendix in Jane's paper, the structure reflects a standard format that has evolved over many years in the *APA Manual*. This format is typical of what you will see when you read research reports in psychology journals that use the APA style. In published articles in APA journals, the author notes, footnotes, tables, and figures are incorporated into the printed text. For a copy manuscript, the APA style stipulates that they be on separate pages in the sequence listed above, and that the caption for a figure be on a separate page preceding the figure. In chapter 8, where we describe how to produce the final manuscript, we give an illustration of a title page that conforms strictly to the APA style for copy manuscripts submitted for publication, but Jane's title page is written for a course she is taking and departs from APA style (as would the title page of a thesis or a dissertation).

Abstract

Although the abstract (or synopsis) appears at the beginning of your report (immediately after the title page), it is actually written after the paper is completed. The abstract provides a concise summary of your report. Think of it as a distillation into one succinct paragraph of the important points covered in the body of the report. In the sample paper in appendix A, Jane summarizes the rationale of her study, what she did, what she found, and its relationship to what she predicted, and she notes that "limitations to the study and suggestions for further research" are also discussed.

When planning your abstract, answer the following questions as concisely as possible:

- What was the objective or purpose of my research study?
- What principal method did I use?
- Who were the research participants?
- What were my major findings?
- What did I conclude from these findings?
- Are there limitations and implications for further research?

More detailed and more specific statements about methods, results, and conclusions are given in the body of your report. The abstract is presented first, and its purpose is to let the reader anticipate what your report is about.

Introduction

The introduction provides the rationale for your research and prepares the reader for the methods you have chosen. Think about the history or background of your topic and how you might go from that kind of opening into your hypotheses or questions. You will be making an evidence-based argument to explain the objective or purpose of your study and what you predicted. Suppose you planned your research as an improvement on a previous study (by X) that had been criticized (by Y) regarding a purported methodological flaw. Stating something like "X (1990) reported an effect of study time, but this experiment was criticized by Y (1992) because of a methodological flaw" would not be good evidence-based writing. The reason is that it fails to adequately describe the effect reported by X and does not identify the methodological flaw that Y criticized. Nor would it be acceptable to present merely a string of loosely related summaries of articles, because you need to show that you understand what you are citing and how it supports a particular view or position.

In her opening paragraph, Jane cites a demographic finding and notes its implications for the importance of her topic. In this way, she develops an evidence-based argument underscoring the value of her research and the logical foundation of her hypotheses. The following paragraphs pick up the thread from her first paragraph. Jane describes succinctly, but in precise detail, what was found in the research she cites. Some students tend to simply assert conclusions advocated by the authors of cited studies and fail to describe the evidence the researchers used to support those assertions. Jane, however, deftly leads into her three hypotheses. She takes nothing for granted and, instead, walks the reader (the instructor) step-by-step through the reasoning behind each hypothesis.

Your literature review might also show the development of your hypotheses or any of your exploratory questions and the reason(s) the research topic seemed worth studying. Strong introductions are those that state the research problem or the hypotheses in such a way that the method section appears to be a natural consequence of that statement. If you can get your readers to think when they later see your method section, "Yes, of course, that's what this researcher had to do to answer this question," then you will have succeeded in writing a strong introduction. Here are some questions to ask yourself as you plan the introduction:

- ◆ What was the purpose of my study?
- ◆ What terms need to be defined?
- ◆ How does my study build on or derive from other studies?
- ◆ What were my hypotheses, predictions, or expectations?

Method

The next step is to think about how you will detail the method used. Frequently, this section is subdivided into "Participants," "Materials," and "Procedure," but no rule states that you must use these subdivisions if you think there is a clearer, more logical, and more fluid way of describing what you did. These are basically the subsections of Jane's method section, except that she calls the third subsection "Design and Procedures." Let's look at each of them.

The first subsection describes the research participants. In a lab experiment, it would be appropriate to give their age and sex, because this information is easily obtained and it may be quite relevant when you discuss the generalizability (called the *external validity*) of the observed results in the discussion section of your report. Most experimenters recruit "opportunity samples"—that is, the first individuals (usually the first students) who are available—rather than use special sampling procedures such as the kind used in polling studies. If you know the age and sex of your subjects, and if the sample sizes are large enough, you may discover that age level or sex is a moderator variable, which would yield an interesting ad hoc hypothesis (a conjecture that you develop on the spot). Psychologists are trained to ask questions about the external validity of research results; thus, your instructor will be thinking about the generalizability of your findings across both persons and settings.

If you plan to include a subsection about the materials that you used, this is the place to describe the tests or standardized measures you used (e.g., validity, reliability) and how you used them. Even if you used well-known, standardized tests, it is still a good idea to describe them in a few sentences, because such a description tells the instructor that you understand the nature and purpose of your measuring instruments. For instance, suppose you used Mark Snyder's Self-Monitoring Scale.[1] In your literature search, you found that research by Briggs, Cheek, and Buss found this instrument to be three-dimensional.[2] In your report, you might say something like:

> The study participants were administered Snyder's 25-item Self-Monitoring Scale (1974). The original purpose of this instrument was to measure self-control and self-observation, but Briggs, Cheek, and Buss (1980) found that the scale actually measures three distinct factors, described by them as extraversion, other-directedness, and acting. *Extraversion* refers to the tendency to be the center of attention in groups; *other-directedness,* to a person's willingness to change his or her behavior to suit others; and *acting,* to liking and being good at speaking and entertaining.

Alternatively, suppose you need to report only the nature of a particular measure and not any follow-up inferences by other researchers. For example, say you used John T. Cacioppo and Richard E. Petty's scale for measuring the need for cognition.[3] You can succinctly describe this measure in a single sentence, if it seems appropriate to do so:

> The participants were administered Cacioppo and Petty's (1982) Need for Cognition Scale, which is an 18-item measure of the tendency to engage in and enjoy thinking.

If you know something about the reliability and validity of the instrument, mention this information as well (along with an appropriate citation), but be specific. It is vague to say only that "the reliability was $r = .50$" without also indicating whether you mean the *test-retest reliability* (the stability of the instrument from one measurement session to another), the *alternate form reliability* (the degree of equivalence of different versions of the instrument), or the *internal-consistency reliability* (the degree of relatedness of individual items or individual components of the instrument when those items or components are used to give a single score). The same rule applies to the reporting of validity findings; tell which type of validity you mean of those described in Exhibit 8.

---

[1] M. Snyder (1974). Self monitoring of expressive behavior. *Journal of Personality and Social Psychology, 30,* 526–537.

[2] S. R. Briggs, J. M. Cheek, & A. H. Buss (1980). An analysis of the self-monitoring scale. *Journal of Personality and Social Psychology, 38,* 679–686.

[3] J. T. Cacioppo & R. E. Petty (1982). The need for cognition. *Journal of Personality and Social Psychology, 42,* 116–131.

EXHIBIT 8 *Uses of the term validity in research and assessment*

construct validity: the degree to which the conceptual variable (or construct) that is presumably measured or studied is what is claimed.

content validity: the adequate sampling of the relevant material or content that a test purports to measure.

criterion validity: the degree to which a measuring instrument is correlated with outcome criteria in the present (its *concurrent validity*) or the future (its *predictive validity*).

external validity: the generalizability of an inferred causal relationship over different people, settings, manipulations, and research outcomes.

face validity: the degree to which a measuring instrument "looks as if" it is measuring something relevant.

internal validity: the soundness of statements about whether one variable is responsible for (i.e., the cause of) a particular outcome.

statistical-conclusion validity: the accuracy of the statistical conclusions drawn.

The final subsection of Jane's method section is where she describes in detail the design of her research and the procedure for implementing it. In planning this section in your report, you will describe all the important aspects of the design and implementation of your study. Did you perform a randomized experiment, and if so, what was the nature of the experimental design (for example, between-subjects or within-subjects, a one-dimensional or a factorial design), and how was the randomization done? If you used some other design, what was it exactly? If you used a quasi-experimental design, did you deal with the problem of nonequivalent groups? If you used a correlational design, what will you have to say (in the discussion section) about the third-variable problem—the possibility that a "third variable" that is correlated with your two main variables is the reason why they were correlated. Other specific issues for you to discuss later in your paper can usually be found in the course text. It is important not to leave out any details whose omission may mislead the reader.

Results

In the next major section, you will describe your findings. Jane begins by telling how she scored the data and operationalized her dependent variable. Afterward, she goes into specific details, beginning with the overall results in each condition. She provides a table of basic summary data, so that an inquisitive reader can recalculate the results. Jane explains why she performed a statistical test that did not address her specific predictions; she did so to check her other calculations, and to demonstrate that she understands certain aspects of other data analyses she reports. Jane's other data analyses are reported next, and in each case, she explains how her hypotheses led her to choose the particular focused statistical tests she used. Jane's discussion of her results—from the most general to the most specific—is, like any good argument, thorough and logically compelling. In chapter 6, we will describe four basic criteria for reporting quantitative information; Jane's results section is an exemplar of all four: (a) clarity, (b) accuracy, (c) precision, and (d) enough detail to allow readers to reach their own conclusions.

We will have more to say about the use of tables and graphics in chapter 6. However, if you plan to include a table or a figure, don't make the reader guess what you are thinking; label your table or figure fully, and discuss the data so it is clear what the results represent. You don't have to repeat every single result from the table or figure in your narrative; but tell what the results mean. Ask yourself the following questions as you structure your results section:

◆ What did I find?
◆ How can I say what I found in a careful, detailed way?
◆ Is what I am planning to say precise and to the point?
◆ Will what I have said be clear to the reader?
◆ Have I left out anything of importance?

A question that students often ask is how precise they should be in reporting statistical tests (such as the t test, the F test, and chi-square), effect sizes, measures of central tendency (such as means and medians), and measures of variability (standard deviations and variances). The rule of thumb is to round the statistical values to two decimal places, as shown in the results section of Jane's report. But in calculating the results, it is essential not to scrimp on the number of decimal places in the intermediate calculations (as illustrated in the appendix of Jane's report, where she shows her calculations). Suppose you are a NASA engineer trying to figure out how much fuel will be needed to complete a manned mission to Mars. Rounding the calculations may send the astronauts on an impossible mission.

Another convention that many students find confusing is how p values are to be presented. Many statisticians recommend reporting the actual descriptive level of significance, because it carries more information than the phrases "significant difference" or "no significant difference at the 5% level." Assuming your instructor does not frown on your reporting p values to more than two or three decimal places, you have several options. One possibility is to list a string of zeros, such as "$p = .00000025$." An alternative (the one used by Jane) is to use scientific notation as a more compact way to show a very small p value. Instead of reporting $p = .00000025$, you report 2.5^{-7}, where the -7 tells the reader to count 7 places to the left of the decimal in 2.5 and make that the decimal place. If you are looking up the p levels in a statistical table, however, your only option may be to state that p is less than ($<$) or greater than ($>$) the particular column value in the statistical table. When you are reporting statistical tests in tables, the *APA Manual* recommends that you use asterisks to identify the probability values (as shown in Jane's Table 2).

Discussion

In the discussion section of your research report, you will form a cohesive unit from the facts you have gathered. Think about how you will discuss your findings in light of how you stated your hypotheses. If you had a sudden insight or an unexpected idea, this is the section of your report in which to discuss it. Incidentally, the name for a lucky discovery is *serendipity;* it is derived from a fairy tale about three princes of Serendip (an ancient name for Sri Lanka) who were constantly making lucky findings. Serendipity is common in everyday life (and also in science) when people keep an open mind that allows them to perceive things in novel ways.[4]

Previously, we mentioned using an evidence-based argument when pulling studies together in the introduction section of your report. In the discussion section, you will make another evidence-based argument, but this time you must try to write "defensively" without being too blatant about it. Be your own devil's advocate and ask yourself what a skeptical reader might see as the other side of your argument or conclusion. Are there shortcomings or inconsistencies, and how might a reader react? All research findings are limited in some ways, but if you cannot find any holes in your argument or conclusion, ask a clever friend to help you out by listening to what you want to argue or conclude in your discussion.

Here are some additional questions to consider as you begin to structure this section:

- What was the purpose of my study?
- How do my results relate to that purpose?
- Were there any serendipitous findings of interest?
- How valid and generalizable are my findings?
- Are there larger implications in these findings?
- Is there an alternative way to interpret my results?

If you believe there are practical or larger implications in your findings, the discussion is the place to spell them out. Are there implications for further research? Some researchers prefer to add a separate section, called "Conclusions," when the discussion is already lengthy and they want to separate the discussion ideas and arguments from some pithy conclusions that may need elaboration. This extra section is usually not necessary if all you have are a few conclusions that you can state in the final paragraph of your discussion section. But in either case, your conclusions should be stated as clearly, accurately, and precisely as possible.

---

[4]A famous example was the inspiration for Velcro fasteners, which happened when a man named George deMestral, while picking cockleburs from his jacket after a stroll in the Swiss countryside, saw that they were covered with hooks that had become embedded in the loops of the fabric of his jacket. A fascinating book on serendipity in science is R. M. Roberts, *Serendipity: Accidental Discoveries in Science* (Wiley, 1989).

References

Once you have made plans for writing the body of the report, think about your reference material again. You will need to include an alphabetized listing of all the sources of information you drew from, and it is essential that every article, chapter, and book (but not personal communications) be listed in your references section. To avoid retracing your steps, keep a running list of the material that will appear in this section as you progress through the early preparation of the report. You can create a separate file called "References" and then copy and paste them into the paper's references section. If at the last minute you find you need to recheck the author, title, or publisher of a particular book, remember that you can go to your library's automated catalog. If you need to check the volume number or pages of a journal article, you can go to PsycINFO for this information.

End Material

In Jane's report, there are an appendix, an author page, a page listing footnotes, and two tables—all following the references section of her paper, and therefore collectively known as the *end material*. The end material in your report might include one or more figures. The APA style is to precede figures by a page of figure titles (called *captions*), but your instructor may be content to have you print the caption under the figure (as shown in John's review paper in appendix B). Some instructors permit students to incorporate the figures within the narrative text, on the assumption that the report is a final manuscript, with the tables and figures appearing as they would in print. This placement will make your report easier to read, but check with your instructor first. The instructor may also permit you to use your word-processing program to automatically insert a footnote or an author note at the bottom of the appropriate page rather than in the end material.

Most instructors like to see the raw materials and computations of the investigation. This is the purpose of the appendix section in Jane's report. Theses and dissertations also generally have an appendix for the raw data and research materials, so that they are available for posterity. Alternatively, some instructors prefer that such information be submitted as a separate package. Had Jane used a questionnaire or test that could not be adequately described in the limited space of the method section, she would have included it here in the appendix of her report. If you used a standard statistical program to analyze your data, your instructor may ask you to make a printout, pare it down to its essentials, and include the pared-down results in the appendix section of your report. Whether or not your instructor requires an appendix, it is important that you save all your notes and raw data until the instructor has returned your research report and you have received a grade in the course—just in case the instructor has questions about your work.

Organizing Your Thoughts

The research report does not usually require a gross outline because its formal structure already provides a skeleton waiting to be fleshed out. Nevertheless, most researchers find it essential to organize their thoughts about each section before writing the first draft. There are several ways to do this:

- ◆ You can scribble on a piece of paper the points you want to cover and, after you have thought about them, make them into a general outline and then a more specific outline. To learn more about outlining, read chapter 5 even though it is recommended for students writing literature reviews; it provides a guide to outlining before or after the fact.
- ◆ You can make notes on separate index cards for each major point you want to cover (for example, the rationale of the study, the derivation of each of your hypotheses, and each background study) and then sort and re-sort these cards until you think you have a clear direction for each section of your first draft.
- ◆ You can also make a computer file of such notes and then cut and paste them back and forth until you think they provide a logical direction for your first draft. However, if there are a lot of these notes, it may be difficult to see the big picture, so you may end up printing the notes on separate pieces of paper and sorting and re-sorting them as you would index cards.

If you are still having a hard time organizing your thoughts, try dictating your ideas into a tape recorder. Take the tape recorder for a walk; tell it what you found in your research. Another possibility is to imagine you are sitting across a table from a friend; tell your "friend" what you found. No matter what approach you favor, make sure that your notes or files are accurate and complete. If you are summarizing or paraphrasing something you read, you must provide the full citation. If you are quoting someone, put the statement in quotation marks, make sure that you have copied it exactly, and write down the page numbers; page numbers are required for an exact quote.

5

Organizing the Review Paper

When you are ready to begin drafting your review paper, the first step is to create a rough outline. The imposition of form will help you collect and refine your thoughts as you shape the paper, and you can prepare a more detailed outline after you have thought some more. But even if you don't outline before you begin the first draft, you should at least do so afterward. If a logical, ordered form does not emerge, the weak spots will become apparent and you can fix them. (If you are writing a research report, and not interested in making an outline, you can skip this chapter and go on to chapter 6.)

Why You Need an Outline

Having submitted a proposal (chapter 4) and thought a lot more about what you've read and the objective of your review paper, you have at least a general idea of what you want to say. Now is the time to crystallize your thoughts into a kind of "road map" leading to the first draft. Without this "map," you may drive yourself to distraction, dissipating the motivation and energy that you need to complete the project on schedule. The name for this map is an outline, and the purpose of this chapter is get you started on creating a coherent, logical, and realistic outline.

A weak structure or a lack of structure is not uncommon in students' reviews; it is often an indication that the student began writing the first draft before preparing a satisfactory outline. One instructor wrote to us, "Some of my students' reviews read like catalogs of studies with no real organization. There's a paragraph on X's study, and then one on Y's study, and then another one on the study by Z." A paper like that is a sure sign that the student did not develop an outline before beginning to write. Without a decent outline, the first draft may ramble on endlessly, and working with it may be like shaking hands with an octopus.

In contrast, if you have a good outline, then you know where your ideas and sentences are heading. For example, you might organize the studies you want to review in chronological order, or group them by the results that supported one hypothesis and then the results that supported an alternative hypothesis, or organize them by methodological features. The more effort you put into outlining your paper, the more informative and persuasive the final product will be—and the more likely you are to complete it on time.

Where to Start

You can begin to organize ideas and studies into a tentative and general outline as you retrieve and read reference material. Use comparison and contrast as a way of categorizing components into groups and subgroups. Add or remove components as you pull together facts, arguments, and studies that document and expand your subtopics. Like an amorphous mass in a science fiction movie that gradually takes shape out of primordial ooze, the structure of even the most incoherent paper will acquire form and shape if you just keep thinking about it patiently.

Your organizing does not have to be done in one sitting, and in fact, it is usually better to take a break, go for a walk, work on something else, and then come back to the problem with a refreshed mind. Your objective is to produce a parallel construction of ideas and a balanced hierarchy of organization that you will expand on and then polish as needed. However, if you find it difficult to get started, there are two tricks you can try:

◆ Think of the outline as a very detailed table of contents based on the headings and subheadings you might want to use in a particular section.
◆ Shop around for an interesting quote that encourages fresh thinking, and if it still seems relevant later on, you can use it to launch the introduction as well as capture and focus the reader's interest.

Before attempting the first draft (discussed in chapter 7), you will need to revise and polish the preliminary outline so that it more precisely reflects the organizational structure of your paper. Even this structure should be viewed not as carved in stone, but as something that can be molded to your ideas as they evolve. Use the structure to guide you, but do not be afraid to change it if your thinking changes.

The Rough Outline

Your first outline can be simply a numbered list of items you want to cover in your paper. You can then think about the list, put it aside for a day or so, and then think about it some more. Asking yourself the following questions should help you get going:

◆ How do I want to begin?
◆ What conclusions do I want to draw?

+ What sections do I need between these two points?
+ In each section, what do I want to emphasize?
+ What illustrations, examples, or quotations can I use?
+ What details do I use? In what order?

Turning again to John Smith's paper in appendix B, you can see that all these questions are addressed. If we could go back a couple of steps and ask how John began structuring his paper, we would find that he might have sketched something like the following:

1. Point out that the concept of intelligence is controversial, that the term is used in more than one way, and that certain accepted assumptions can be explained in other ways.
2. Raise the issue that assessing intelligence is not without potential problems.
3. Review the history of the traditional (*g*-centered) theoretical orientation and what I call the multiplex orientation.
4. Explain Gardner's theory of multiple intelligences.
5. Review point-counterpoint criticisms and rejoinders.
6. Sum up the main ideas and say something about further research.

There is enough here to let John think about the fine details of each section and frame a more meticulous outline. In getting down to specifics, he needs to keep all of his ideas parallel to ensure logical consistency in his arguments. Just as the rough outline can take different forms, the detailed outline that John next constructs can be set down in topics, sentences, or paragraphs—whichever seems to make the most sense as his ideas begin to flow.

Making Ideas Parallel

For the more detailed outline, whether you decide to work with topics, sentences, or paragraphs, the form you choose should be the only one that you use. In other words, you need to make the ideas parallel. In the following outline fragment, the ideas are clearly not parallel:

I. What is intelligence? What does "*g*-centric" mean? What will follow?
II. Two views
    A. Traditional—the general overriding factor of intelligence is measured by every task on an intelligence test
    B. Spearman's psychometric contribution
    C. Developmental psychologists, following Piaget, argue for general mental structures
    D. *The Bell Curve*

The problem is that this outline is a hodgepodge of questions, topics, idea fragments, and a book title. Working with this jumble will be like swimming upstream. Such an outline will sabotage your efforts to put thoughts and notes into a logical sequence. Contrast this incoherent structure with the parallel structure of the following outline:

    I. Two views of intelligence
        A. The traditional approach
            1. General overriding trait (Spearman)
                a. "g-centric" notion of intelligence
                b. Jensen and heritability
            2. Piaget's idea of general structures of the mind
                a. Universal developmental sequence
                b. Biological operationalization (speed of neural transmission)
            3. Herrnstein and Murray's book on role of g in society

What makes the second outline an improvement over the first is not only that the same form is used throughout but that the ideas are also logically ordered. The second outline looks more polished and inviting and will certainly be easier to use as a writing plan.

Putting Ideas in Order

To create this polished look, whether you use topics, sentences, or paragraphs for your detailed outline, the trick is to try to group your information in descending order, from the most general facts or ideas to the most specific details and examples. You can see this approach clearly in the parallel format of the second outline shown above.

The rule of orderly precision applies whether you are outlining definitions, the nature of a particular theory, evaluation criteria, or a series of arguments and counterarguments. You can see the order and precision in the following outline segment:

    II. Gardner's theory of "intelligences"
        A. Definition of intelligence
            1. Problem solving and creative abilities
            2. Evaluation criteria
                a. Isolation if brain-damaged
                b. Existence of exceptional populations
                c. Unique core operations
                d. Distinctive developmental history
                e. Existence of primitive antecedents
                f. Openness to experimentation
                g. Prediction of performance on tests
                h. Accessibility of information content
        B. Kinds of intelligence
            1. Logical-mathematical
            2. Linguistic
            3. Spatial

EXHIBIT 9 *Subdivision of the outline*

I.
   A.
   B.
      1.
      2.
         a.
         b.
            (1)
            (2)
               (a)
               (b)
II.

    4. Bodily-kinesthetic
    5. Musical
    6. Personal
       a. Intrapersonal
       b. Interpersonal

    Another convention in making a detailed outline, as illustrated in Exhibit 9, is that if there is a subtopic division, there should be at least two subtopics, never only one. Facts, ideas, and concepts are classified by the use of Roman numerals (I, II, III); capitals (A, B, C); Arabic numerals (1, 2, 3); lowercase letters (a, b, c); and finally, numbers and letters in parentheses. Thus, if you list I, you should list II (and perhaps III and IV and so on); if A, then B; if 1, then 2.

    The Roman numerals indicate the outline's main ideas. Indented capital letters provide main divisions within each main idea. The letters and numbers that follow list the supporting details and examples. Note the indentation of each subtopic. Any category can be expanded to fit the number of supporting details or examples that you wish to cover in the paper. Any lapses in logic are bound to surface if you use this system of organization, so you can catch and correct them before proceeding.

    For example, look at the following abbreviated outline; item B is clearly a conspicuous lapse in logic:

    II. Gardner's theory of "intelligences"
       A. His definition of intelligence
       B. How did the concept of *g* originate?
       C. Seven kinds of intelligence

    Item B should be moved from this section of the outline to the one pertaining to the *g*-centric view of intelligence. Some items may require a return to PsycINFO or the library to clarify a point or to supplement parts of the outline with additional reference material.

Template for Writing and Note Taking

The outline is a way not only to organize your thoughts but also to make it easier to start writing. If you use the phrase or sentence format, the paper will almost write itself, as we see clearly in the following outline fragment:

II. Gardner's theory of "intelligences"
  A. Definition of intelligence
    1. "the ability to solve problems, or to create products that are valued within one or more cultural settings" (Gardner, 1983, p. x)
    2. Intellectual talent must satisfy eight criteria (Gardner, 1983)
      a. Possible identification of intelligences by damage to particular areas of the brain
      b. Existence of exceptional populations (savants), implying the distinctive existence of a special entity

Had our hypothetical outline used complete sentences, the paper would write itself:

II. Gardner's theory of "intelligences"
  A. Definition of intelligence
    1. Gardner (1983) conceived of intelligence as "the ability to solve problems, or to create products that are valued within one or more cultural settings" (p. x).
    2. Gardner (1983) argued that a talent must fit eight criteria to be considered "intelligence."
      a. There is potential to isolate the intelligence by brain damage.
      b. Exceptional populations (e.g., savants) provide evidence of distinct entities.

In chapter 2, we alluded to one other helpful hint about preparing an outline. The outline's coding system makes it convenient to code the notes you take during your literature search. If your notes refer to section "II.B.1" of your outline, then you will record this code on the card, photocopy, or computer printout. In this way, order is brought to your notes. If you are using cards, for example, you can spread them on a large table and sort through them according to the section from your notes and the outline, each component enhancing the other.

Keep in mind, however, that the outline is only a guide. Its specific structure may change as you integrate your notes.

Tricks to Get You Started

Some students find it difficult to write an outline because the ideas are not yet really organized in their thinking. Here are a couple of tricks you can try in order to focus your thinking:

- One technique that you may have learned in high school English is called *clustering*. You draw a circle and write in the central

EXHIBIT 10 A preliminary cluster outline

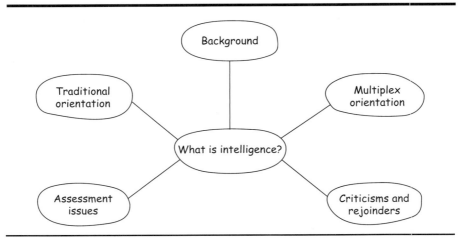

question or theme of your paper, and then add more circles to represent major subdivisions. (Exhibit 10 shows such a cluster based on John Smith's paper.) The final cluster will represent the fine differentiations that you make by adding spokes and circles until it all makes sense to you.

- Another technique is to write the tentative section headings on index cards, which you then move back and forth until you think they are in the right logical order. Then write each study or idea on a separate index card, and sort these cards below the appropriate section headings. You can color-code the various cards to represent possible headings, subheadings, and so forth.

Outlining After the Fact

Some students write their papers over more than one semester (a senior thesis, for example) and may feel they cannot outline from the outset because they do not know where the final paper will go. When they do sit down to write, they tend to incorporate material from their earlier drafts, but they do not make an outline first. Still other students find the process of making an outline too exacting, preferring instead to sit at the computer and let the stream of ideas flow spontaneously.

If either case describes you, then try outlining after the fact. To assure yourself that your work has what psychologists call a *good gestalt* (a coherent, psychologically appealing form), make a "mini-table-of-contents" of your final draft, and then do a more detailed outline within the headings and subheadings. Outlining features are also available on the word processor. Ask yourself:

- Is my discussion focused, and do the ideas flow from or build on one another?
- Have I amply developed each idea?
- Have I provided supporting details for each main idea discussed?
- Are the ideas balanced?
- Is my writing to the point, or have I gone off on a tangent?

An experienced writer working with a familiar topic might be able to achieve success without a detailed outline. For others, the lack of an outline often creates havoc and frustration, not to mention wasted time and effort. If you would like to practice on someone else's work, try outlining some section of John's paper. Ask yourself how well his discussion addresses the five preceding questions. If you find problems in the structure of his discussion, think of ways that he could have avoided them or corrected them before he submitted the paper.

6

Communicating Statistical Information

Whether you are citing someone else's quantitative results in a review paper or describing your own detailed statistical analysis in a research report, the information should be presented clearly, accurately, precisely, and in enough detail to allow readers to reach their own conclusions. (If you will not be presenting any statistical information, you can skip this chapter and go on to chapter 7.)

Four Guidelines: CAPE

This chapter is for students who have taken an introductory course in statistics or are currently taking one, and who need to report statistical results in a literature review or a research report. In his review paper, John Smith quotes a researcher's statement that "approximately three fourths of the variance in real-world performance is not accounted for by intelligence test performance." In his footnote 3, John properly notes that "finding a predictor variable that accounts for approximately one quarter of the variance (i.e., an effect size correlation of around .5) is not unimpressive in psychological research," and he cites a supporting reference (suggested to him by his instructor, whom he thanks in his author note section). Some review papers, called *meta-analyses* (meaning the "analysis of analyses"), consist primarily of the use of statistical and graphical methods to sum up numerous studies that address essentially the same question. If you are getting ready to write a research report, you know that detailed statistical analyses are considered an important part of the results section, as Jane Doe's report illustrates. (To help jog your memory of common statistical terms, Exhibit 11 lists some of the most popular ones and their definitions.)

Although the information presented by Jane is the kind that is supposed to be routinely reported in journal articles, not every researcher provides all these details. For example, not always reported are effect sizes, although

EXHIBIT 11 *Common statistical abbreviations and symbols*

Symbol/ abbreviation	*Definition*
English symbols/abbreviations	
ANOVA	Acronym for *analysis of variance,* a statistical procedure in which the total variance of a set of scores is partitioned into its components and *F* tests are used to statistically evaluate the difference between variances.
CI	Confidence interval (i.e., the upper and lower bounds of a statistic), with the confidence level defined as $1 - \alpha$ (i.e., the probability that the range of values will contain the population value of the statistic).
d	Cohen's effect size index for the difference between two independent means, a descriptive value calibrated in standard score (*z*-score) units ranging from zero to positive or negative infinity.
df	Degrees of freedom.
F	Fisher's test of significance in ANOVA is used to evaluate the tenability of the null hypothesis of no difference between two or more means or variances.
g	Hedges's effect size index for the difference between two independent means, an inferential value calibrated in standard score (*z*-score) units ranging from zero to positive or negative infinity.
M	The simple arithmetic average of a set of scores (i.e., the arithmetic mean).
Mdn	The median, or midmost score of a distribution.
MS	The unbiased estimate of the population variance, also symbolized as S^2.
n	The number of scores or observations in one condition or subgroup of a study.
N	The total number of scores or observations in a study.
p level	The probability of rejecting the null hypothesis when it is true (i.e., the probability of a Type I error).
r	Pearson product-moment correlation, an index of the linear relation between a pair of variables.
SD	Standard deviation, an index of the variability of a set of data around the mean value in a sample.
SS	The sum of the squared deviations from the mean in a set of scores.
t	A test of significance used to judge the tenability of the null hypothesis of no relation between two variables.
z score	Score converted to a standard deviation unit.
Greek symbols/abbreviations	
α	Alpha, the probability of a Type I error (i.e., the error of rejecting the null hypothesis when it is true), where $1 - \alpha$ is the confidence level. (The term alpha is also used to describe a measure of internal consistency reliability, known as *Cronbach's alpha.*)
β	Beta, the probability of a Type II error (i.e., the error of failing to reject the null hypothesis when it is false), where $1 - \beta$ (the probability of not making a Type II error) refers to the power of a statistical test.

EXHIBIT 11 *Continued*

λ	Lambda, a value in a set of coefficients (λ weights) that sum to zero and are used to state a prediction (illustrated in Jane Doe's research report in appendix A).
σ	The standard deviation of a population of scores.
σ^2	The variance of a population of scores.
Σ	Instruction telling us to sum (add) a set of scores.
φ	Phi coefficient, the Pearson *r* where both variables are dichotomous.
χ^2	Chi-square, a statistic used to test the degree of agreement between the frequency data obtained and the frequency data expected under a particular hypothesis (e.g., the null hypothesis).

the *APA Manual* states that, because the probability value does not directly reflect the magnitude of an effect or the strength of a relationship, "it is almost always necessary to include some index of effect size or strength of relationship in your Results section." We will have more to say about the distinction between the probability value and the effect size, but fortunately, as meta-analysts have discovered, there are ways of ferreting out effect sizes (and other missing statistical details) from the barest available raw ingredients. This chapter emphasizes four general guidelines for reporting statistical information, designated by the acronym *CAPE,* which stands for *c*larity, *a*ccuracy, *p*recision, and *e*nough detail to enable readers to make their own inferences. At the conclusion of the chapter are recommended readings, including "how-to" articles that illustrate data-analytic procedures and also provide guidance on their use.

Reporting Results Clearly

Clarity of reporting means not obfuscating details in obscure or murky visual displays, or using technical terms inappropriately because you do not fully understand them, or reporting a diffuse analysis although you hypothesized a specific result (but never actually evaluated it statistically). Check with the instructor to get expert feedback on the graphics, technical terms, and analyses you want to use. (We will have more to say about diffuse statistical tests later on in this discussion.) It is also extremely important that the structure of your paper enable the reader to easily follow the logic of your reasoning. Writing the proposal (chapter 3) was your initial attempt to develop a coherent structure. If you are writing a research report, the traditional structure in chapter 4 is designed to impose coherence on the presentation. If your assignment is to write a review paper, the guidelines in chapter 5 should help you develop a good outline before you begin writing the first draft.

With the advent of computer graphics, it is easy to be lulled into a false sense of security about the clarity and interpretability of figures that take the form of line graphs, bar graphs, pie charts, shaded maps, and so on. The *APA Manual* advises the use of figures when you want to "convey at a quick glance an overall pattern of results," on the assumption that the figure actually communicates details in a more efficient way than you can express them in words. Whether you are using a figure (as in John's review paper) or tables (as in Jane's research report), you need to mention their existence and interpret them.

If you are using figures, the *APA Manual*'s criteria for creating good figures are simplicity, clarity, and continuity. These are some additional guidelines:

- Use the figure to enhance what you say in the narrative text, that is, by supplementing or expanding on it.
- Don't encumber a figure with superfluous data or distracting details; it should be easy to understand, communicating only essential facts.
- Use font, lines, labels, and symbols that are large enough, and easy enough to see, so the figure can be read easily.
- Use the same lettering in all figures, so the reader is not put off by different styles.
- The data should be precisely plotted. If you are drawing a figure by hand, use graph paper to keep the rows and columns evenly spaced, and then reduce the figure and paste it into your report.
- When displaying the relationship between an independent and a dependent variable (or between a predictor variable and a criterion or outcome variable) in a line graph or bar graph, it is customary to put the independent (or predictor) variable on the horizontal axis (the *x*-axis, or abscissa) and the dependent (or criterion) variable on the vertical axis (the *y*-axis, or ordinate).
- The units should progress from small to large.

In his book *Elements of Graph Design,* Harvard University psychologist Stephen M. Kosslyn wrote on how the brain perceives and processes visual information and what the implications are for visual displays. (Kosslyn's book is listed in the annotated bibliography at the end of this chapter.) As an illustration, Kosslyn concluded that we are rarely aware of complex spatial relations between parts of a display because of how the human brain has developed. Thus, it is frequently better to report complex data in a table, particularly if you want to communicate exact relations. Of course, another good reason for tables is that exact values can be provided; when the data are summarized in figures, readers can make only an educated guess about exact values.

If you plan to use color, Kosslyn offered the following tips:

- Choose colors that are well separated in the spectrum, because those close together are harder to discriminate. The colors perceived as being most separated are reddish purple, blue, yellowish gray, yellowish green, red, and bluish gray.
- Colors that, according to popular wisdom, are never confused (unless the person is color-blind) are white, gray, black, red, green, yellow, blue, pink, brown, orange, and purple.

- Use only a few of these colors, however, because using a lot of colors in the same visual display can confuse the reader.
- Avoid juxtaposing red (which has a relatively long wavelength) and blue (which has a relatively short wavelength), as they may be perceived as shimmering.
- Avoid cobalt blue, which is actually a mixture of blue and red and is hard to keep in focus. As an example, you may recall seeing a halo around blue streetlights at night, and you may have thought it was due to fog; it was a visual phenomenon caused by your eyes' inability to focus the image properly.

Kosslyn summed up the psychological basis of graph design in the following three principles:

1. *The mind is not a camera.* That is, we do not see things only as they are. The baggage we bring to every situation, such as experiential factors and expectancies, comes into play. You remember the old proverb that "seeing is believing," but it is also true that believing is seeing, in that people tend to perceive in ways that fit into their expectations.
2. *The mind judges a book by its cover.* That is, people take appearance as a clue to reality. As an extreme example, imagine a figure that reports the results of two teams, called the Blue Team and the Red Team, but the graph uses blue ink to represent the Red Team and red ink to represent the Blue Team. This figure will inevitably create confusion, because the mind gravitates to physical appearance—in this case, to the color of the ink to infer the meaning of the words written in it.
3. *The spirit is willing, but the mind is weak.* That is, the visual and memory systems have natural limitations, which must be respected if visual displays are to be interpreted correctly.

Reporting Results Accurately

The second guideline requires the candid reporting of statistical results, not bending the facts by omitting relevant details or painting a picture that varies from what was observed. Accuracy also means making a conscientious effort to avoid mistakes in recording and calculation, in other words, checking your measurements, calculations, and numbers. Checking the raw data is a way to spot statistical outliers, the name for scores that lie far outside the normal range. Should you identify any, make sure they are not recording mistakes. Once you know that the scores are recorded accurately, you may decide to report not only the means, but also medians as insurance against misleading interpretations. For example, suppose you want to describe the average income of a group of 10 people, and 9 of them are clustered together but the remaining person is far out on the scale. The median is not affected by the intrusion of this person's far-out income. Of course, it is prudent to report the range of incomes or some other measure of spread, so that readers are not misled into inferring that all 10 people are clustered together.

Accuracy also means being candid about when you formulated your hypotheses and predictions and not pretending that a hypothesis you developed once you inspected the data was conceived before you saw the data. There is an old Bohemian legend about a fabled archer, known throughout the land. One day, the king comes upon the archer standing next to a grove of trees. Each tree has a chalked circle and an arrow in the exact center of the circle. "Teach me to become a great marksman like yourself and I will give you an empire," the king tells the archer. "Keep your empire," the honest archer replies, "for the secret of my skill is that I shoot first and draw the circle afterward." Similarly, accuracy and honesty require that you inform readers which came first, inspecting the data or coming up with a prediction, because very little skill is required to come up with a "prediction" *after* you have inspected the data.

Accuracy and clarity frequently seem to be confounded, because the accurate reporting of information means describing a study in a way that is transparent rather than vague, including its design, conduct, analysis, and interpretation. As a case in point, randomized clinical trials (RCTs) in medical research have been criticized as being vague in the reporting of vital details about how the subjects or patients were allocated to groups or conditions. Despite educational efforts to correct this problem, it seems that many medical studies continue to report information in an ambiguous way that can result in biased estimates of the effectiveness of the clinical treatments.[1]

This case is also a reminder that inaccuracy is not only wasteful of resources but can be demoralizing as well, because biased conclusions and the misleading recommendations that result may lead to false hopes. You may be wondering, however, what all this has to do with your research, as you are not conducting a clinical trial. The answer is that, whatever the nature of your study, a scientific imperative is to describe the design, implementation, data analysis, and your interpretation of the results fully and accurately.

Another way in which inaccuracy is wasteful of resources is a common problem. It might be described as "missing the forest for the *p*" because it concerns how *p* values can cloud students' perceptions. We will have more to say about *p* values again in this chapter, but the point is not to behave as if there were some special place in the instructor's heart for students with *p* values less than .05, or to think that a nonsignificant *p* is evidence that the effect size is zero. Your instructor will admire a "statistically nonsignificant" result as much as a "statistically significant" result, as long as the data are reported accurately and honestly, and appropriate implications are drawn.

---

[1]Discussed in D. Moher, K. R. Schulz, & D. G. Altman (2001). The CONSORT statement: Revised recommendations for improving the quality of reports of parallel-group randomized trials. *Annals of Internalized Medicine, 134,* 657–662.

Reporting Results Precisely

Diffuse and precise statistical tests are technically referred to as *omnibus tests* and *focused tests,* respectively. An easy way to distinguish between them is to remember that all t tests, F tests with 1 degree of freedom in the numerator, and chi-square (χ^2) tests with 1 degree of freedom are focused, whereas all F tests with more than 1 degree of freedom in the numerator and all χ^2 tests with more than 1 degree of freedom are omnibus significance tests. Focused tests not only are more precise but usually are more powerful than omnibus significance tests as well; for this reason, focused significance tests are recommended for evaluating exact experimental predictions.

We presume that the significance test you use is specifically addressed to your working hypothesis. If you use the wrong significance test or fail to pay heed to statistical power considerations, you may end up letting go of your working hypothesis prematurely, perhaps without even realizing it. If you know the old Tarzan movies, where he swings from tree to tree, you may also know that Tarzan was originally played by Johnny Weissmuller. When he was asked his philosophy of life, Weissmuller's response was that "the main thing is not to let go of the vine." This is good advice for student researchers as well: Know what you predicted, and hang onto it long enough to test your hypothesis.

Finally, in reporting results precisely and candidly, try to strike a balance between being discursive and being falsely or needlessly precise. *False precision* means that something that is inherently vague is reported in overly exact terms. Suppose you used a standard attitude questionnaire in your research, and the subjects responded on a 5-point scale from "strongly agree" to "strongly disagree." It would be false precision to report the means to a high number of decimal places, because your measuring instrument was not that sensitive to slight variations in attitudes. *Needless precision* means reporting the results more exactly than the circumstances require. Suppose you are reporting the weight of mouse subjects to six decimal places. Although your measuring instrument may be capable of this precision, the situation does not call for such exactitude. When in doubt, ask the instructor for guidance.

Reporting Enough Information

Earlier in this chapter, we mentioned the *APA Manual*'s recommendation "to include some index of effect size or strength of relationship in your Results section." *Effect size* is actually a general term that may, for example, refer to the difference in outcomes in two groups, or to the magnitude of the relationship between membership in these groups and scores on the dependent variable, or to a ratio of the odds of obtaining a particular outcome depending on the treatment condition. There are subtleties and nuances in the use of these and other effect size indicators (there are discussions in the list of recommended readings). The principal point, however, is that there are many ways of conceptualizing the effect size.

One useful effect size indicator in psychology is the Pearson product-moment correlation (r), which is used to indicate the strength of association between a predictor and a dependent variable, with $r_{\text{effect size}} = 1$ indicating a perfect linear relationship, and $r_{\text{effect size}} = 0$ indicating that neither variable can be predicted from the other by use of a linear equation. A positive r tells us that an increase in scores on one variable is associated with an increase in scores on the other variable, whereas a negative r indicates that an increase in scores on one variable is associated with a decrease in scores on the other variable.

Another popular effect size measure is Cohen's d; it indicates the standardized difference between two group means (resembling a z score), with values ranging from zero to positive or negative infinity. Cohen's d of 0 would imply that normal distributions of the populations underlying the two groups are perfectly superimposed on one another, and $d = .8$ (Cohen called this a "large effect") would imply that the amount of nonoverlap is 47.4%. Your research methods text should contain further information about effect sizes and how they are computed and interpreted.

There are good reasons to report the effect size, not just the p level of your significance test. One reason is that the p level depends a lot on the size of the sample. It is quite possible for the same magnitude of effect to be "significant" or "nonsignificant" depending on the number of sampling units (e.g., subjects) in your study. The following table lists correlations (think of each r below as an effect size correlation) significant at $p = .05$ (two-tailed), given the particular "$N - 2$" value (which refers to the degrees of freedom, defined here as the total sample size minus 2):

$N - 2$	r	$N - 2$	r
1	.997	40	.304
2	.950	50	.273
3	.878	100	.195
4	.811	200	.138
5	.754	300	.113
10	.576	500	.088
20	.423	1,000	.062
30	.349	2,000	.044

This table explains why the p value, alone, does not tell us whether the observed effect was small or large, because all the correlations (the r values) in this table are significant at $p = .05$ (two-tailed). Notice that what counts most in the table is that the total sample size was sufficiently large to enable the r in question to be detected at this p level. Notice also that a correlation that is as small as $r = .044$ is significant at $p = .05$ with $N = 2,002$, but that an r thirteen times larger is *not* statistically significant at the same p level with $N = 12$. Stating only that "the observed effect was statistically significant" would not give the reader any clue to the size of the effect.

Another way of thinking about significance testing and effect size is summarized by the following conceptual equation:

$$\text{Significance test} = \text{Effect size} \times \text{Study size},$$

which explains that significance tests (e.g., t, F, or χ^2) can be parsed into two components, one of which is a reflection of the size of the effect, and the other, the size of the study (e.g., the number of sampling units). You have been taught that the larger the value of the significance test (that is, the bigger the t, F, or χ^2), the smaller (and usually more coveted) the p value.

For example, when the sample sizes of two independent groups that are being compared by a t test are equal ($n_1 = n_2$), one way to describe an independent-sample t test in the style of the conceptual equation above is

$$t = d \times \frac{\sqrt{df}}{2}$$

where df in this case is usually the total sample size minus 2. Notice that the effect size indicator in this example is Cohen's d, which can be estimated by

$$d = \frac{M_1 - M_2}{\sigma_{\text{pooled}}}$$

where the difference between two group means (M_1 and M_2) is divided by the pooled population standard deviation.

The implication is that the value of t will increase as the difference between means M_1 and M_2 increases, as variability within the groups (i.e., the σ_{pooled}) decreases, and as the total sample size increases. If you were designing an experiment, you might try to maximize your test statistic by (a) selecting the strongest manipulation ethically and practically feasible, because that would drive the means further apart; (b) choosing a relatively homogeneous sample of subjects and a standardized procedure, because that would minimize the variability within the groups; and/or (c) recruiting as many subjects as you can afford or as are practical to run, because that increases the study size.

As we said, the product-moment r and Cohen's d are not the only effect size indicators used in research in psychology. Furthermore, the product-moment r comes in different forms. For example, the point-biserial correlation (r_{pb}) is a Pearson r that indexes the strength of association between a dichotomous variable (*biserial* means two sets of measures, such as male gender vs. female gender, or control group vs. experimental group) and a continuous variable (*point* means a value on a continuum). The phi coefficient (ϕ) is a Pearson r that is used to measure the degree of association between two dichotomous variables. In the appendix section of Jane Doe's report, she notes that she computed another effect size correlation, r_{alerting}, which takes its name from the fact that squaring it (i.e., r^2_{alerting}) "alerts" us to the proportion of between-conditions sum of squares that could be accounted for by her linear contrast weights. Because there are different effect size indices, and thus different ranges, always tell which effect size index you used.

The *APA Manual* also advises that, whenever possible, researchers report confidence intervals for population estimates such as means, proportions, and effect sizes. The confidence interval tells us the upper and lower estimated bounds of the population value; the confidence level (defined as $1 - \alpha$) indicates how "approximate" the estimation is. Thus, 95% confidence tells us we can be 95% sure that the population value we are trying to estimate falls between those lower and upper limits.[2] If you increase the level of confidence—say, from 95% to 99%—you widen the confidence interval. Similarly, reducing the level of confidence from 95% to 90% shrinks the confidence interval. To understand why this is so, think of how wide an interval you would need to be 100% sure about some risky event.

Before we leave this discussion of "how much information is enough," the following checklist will serve as a reminder of the statistical information recommended in the *APA Manual:*

- ◆ Report the values of your test statistics (e.g., t, F, χ^2), their degrees of freedom (df), and the probability (p) of obtaining values as extreme as or more extreme than the value of each test statistic.
- ◆ Particularly in the case of t tests (and z tests), it is also important to indicate whether the p value is directional (one-tailed) or nondirectional (two-tailed).
- ◆ Report the effect sizes of all focused tests (i.e., t tests, F tests with numerator $df = 1$, and $1 - df \chi^2$ tests), and interpret the effect sizes in the context of your study and of the variables you are measuring.
- ◆ Report the confidence intervals of means, proportions, and effect sizes,[3] and interpret the results accordingly.
- ◆ Report sample sizes and measures of variability.
- ◆ Pay heed to statistical power, particularly if you are reporting a significance test that was not statistically significant (see Jane's discussion section for an illustration).

Pentimento

If you are writing a review paper, then you know that not all the information above is routinely reported in journal articles. However, as mentioned earlier, even when statistical information is missing, there may be a way of simulating or re-creating it from the barest of ingredients. For example, one of the recommended readings below describes how to estimate effect sizes in experimental

---

[2]This view of what a confidence interval tells us reflects an approach that is called *Bayesian.* There are other ways of thinking about confidence intervals that are also correct, although the Bayesian interpretation is perhaps closest to what people are likely to do in their everyday analyses of data.

[3]The estimation of confidence intervals for effect sizes in association with nonindependent means is a matter of debate, although there are certainly procedures you can use to display and interpret the effect size; see, for example, pp. 308–309 in R. L. Rosnow & R. Rosenthal (2008). *Beginning Behavioral Research: A Conceptual Primer,* 6th ed. (Pearson Prentice Hall).

studies from just the reported sample sizes and a precise p value (see Rosenthal and Rubin's $r_{equivalent}$ statistic). The novelist Lillian Hellman wrote a book entitled *Pentimento*, a term that she borrowed from art restoration and that refers to the reappearance of a hidden image, usually one that has been painted over. As paintings age, the old paint tends to become transparent, and sometimes almost translucent, and we may begin to perceive something beneath the surface. Similarly, for students skilled enough in statistical reasoning and enterprising enough to want to explore the data further, useful information is waiting to be restored beneath the surface of research reports. Further discussion of this topic is beyond the scope of this book, but we mention it to whet your curiosity and interest, because its pursuit can be as much fun as solving a good mystery story.

Recommended Readings

For more about the topics discussed in this chapter, the most readily accessible source is your statistics or research methods text and its Web page links. Encyclopedias in psychology and related areas are often a source of general information, such as A. E. Kazdin's *Encyclopedia of Psychology* (Oxford University Press & American Psychological Association, 2000), N. J. Smelser and P. B. Baltes's *International Encyclopedia of the Social and Behavioral Sciences* (Elsevier, 2002), and M. Lewis-Beck, A. E. Bryman, and T. F. Liao's *Sage Encyclopedia of Social Science Methods* (Sage, 2004). Definitions of many statistical terms used in psychology can be found in the *APA Dictionary of Psychology*.

The readings described below were selected on the basis of their accessibility to college students. Articles with how-to instructions or illustrations are denoted by an asterisk (*), and the numbered readings indicate the suggested sequence in which they should be read:

Significance Testing and Statistical Power

1. Cohen, J. (1990). Things I have learned (so far). *American Psychologist, 45,* 1304–1312. Description by the late Jacob Cohen of the role of statistical power in null hypothesis significance testing (NHST) and laments that so many researchers who engage in NHST pay little attention to power and, as a consequence, frequently end up handicapping themselves without even realizing it.

*Hallahan, M., & Rosenthal, R. (1996). Statistical power: Concepts, procedures, and applications. *Behaviour Research and Therapy, 34,* 489–499. Ten ways of increasing statistical power.

*Killeen, P. R. (2005). An alternative to null-hypothesis significance tests. *Psychological Science, 16,* 345–353. Discussion of an interesting new statistic, called p_{rep}, proposed by Killeen as an alternative to NHST when the ability to replicate a research finding is of primary interest, where replication is defined as "an effect of the same sign as that found in the original experiment" (p. 346).

Effect Size Indicators

*1. Rosnow, R. L., & Rosenthal, R. (2003). Effect sizes for experimenting psychologists. *Canadian Journal of Experimental Psychology, 57,* 221–237. Description of three families of effect size indicators in a variety of cases, and the interpretation as well as the limitations of particular effect size indices such as the odds ratio, relative risk, and risk difference in clinical trials.

*2. Rosenthal, R., & Rubin, D. B. (2003). $r_{equivalent}$: A simple effect size estimator. *Psychological Methods, 8,* 492–496. Description of how to ferret out a point-biserial effect size r from the total sample size (N) and the exact p value, a procedure that is especially useful in reporting nonparametric statistics for which there are accurate p values but effect size indices have not yet been developed (such as the Mann-Whitney U test).

*Rosnow, R. L., Rosenthal, R., & Rubin, D. B. (2000). Contrasts and correlations in effect-size estimation. *Psychological Science, 11,* 446–453. Formulas that you can use with a calculator for computing Cohen's d and Hedges's g from independent-sample t tests, and for converting g into r. There is also a formula for estimating the loss of power in unequal-n designs relative to equal-n designs. Effect size correlations for use with focused statistical tests on more than two independent groups are also explained.

Confidence and Null-Counternull Intervals

Fidler, F., Thomason, N., Cumming, G., Finch, S., & Leeman, J. (2004). Editors can lead researchers to confidence intervals, but can't make them think: Statistical reform lessons from medicine. *Psychological Science, 15,* 119–126. Discussion of the traditional routine reporting of confidence intervals in medical journals (also recommended in the *APA Manual*) and their failure to become standard in psychology. To download a PDF copy of this article (and other instructive articles and modules), visit Professor Geoff Cumming's Web site at La Trobe University, Australia, at http://www.latrobe.edu.au/psy/esci/index.html.

*Masson, E. J., & Loftus, G. R. (2003). Using confidence intervals for graphically based data interpretations. *Canadian Journal of Experimental Psychology, 57,* 203–220. Illustration of the use of confidence intervals in figures and graphs (as in Jane Doe's Figure 1 in appendix A).

*Rosenthal, R., & Rubin, D. B. (1994). The counternull value of an effect size: A new statistic. *Psychological Science, 5,* 329–334. Discussion of how the counternull statistic, which is conceptually related to confidence intervals, involves the obtained effect size and the null hypothesis and is insurance against prematurely believing the null hypothesis to be true when the p value exceeds .05.

Meta-Analysis and Focused Statistical Tests

Hunt, M. (1997). *How science takes stock: The story of meta-analysis.* New York: Russell Sage Foundation. The story of how meta-analysis originated for the purpose of reconciling the differences and validating the generalizations of numerous experiments that address essentially the same scientific question.

Rosenthal, R., & DiMatteo, M. R. (2001). Meta-analysis: Recent developments in quantitative methods for literature reviews. *Annual Review of Psychology, 52,* 59–82. Introduction to meta-analysis that addresses basic questions concerning its use to summarize related studies and to identify variables that moderate observed relationships.

*Rosnow, R. L., & Rosenthal, R. (1996). Computing contrasts, effect sizes, and counternulls on other people's published data: General procedures for research consumers. *Psychological Methods, 1,* 331–340. Statistical procedures for computing focused *t*, *F*, and *z* tests on more than two independent groups, as well as their interpretation by Cohen's *d*, Hedges's *g*, and the Pearson *r* and the construction of confidence limits and the null-counternull interval.

Figures, Graphs, and Other Visual Displays

The following are three advanced discussions of the presentation of graphical information, whether you are writing a paper for a course assignment or have left the academic ivory tower and entered the world of business or government:

*Kosslyn, S. M. (1994). *Elements of graph design.* New York: W. H. Freeman.

*Tufte, E. R. (2001). *The visual display of quantitative information* (2nd ed.). Cheshire, CT: Graphics Press.

*Wainer, H., & Thissen, D. (1993). Graphical data analysis. In G. Keren & C. Lewis (Eds.), *A handbook for data analysis in the behavioral sciences* (pp. 391–457). Hillsdale, NJ: Erlbaum.

7

Writing
and Polishing

Writing a first draft is a little like taking the first dip in chilly ocean waters on a hot day. It may be uncomfortable at the outset but feels better once you get used to it. In this chapter, we provide some pointers to buoy you up as you begin writing.

Sorting Through Your Material

Back in 1947, there was a fascinating story in newspapers and magazines about two brothers, the Collyers, who were found dead in a rubbish-filled mansion at Fifth Avenue and 128th Street in New York City. On receiving a tip that one brother, Homer Collyer, had died, the police forced their way into the mansion with crowbars and axes. They found all of the entrances to the house blocked by wrapped packages of newspapers, hundreds of cartons, and all kinds of junk (14 grand pianos, most of a Model T Ford, the top of a horse-drawn carriage, a tree limb 7 feet long and 20 inches in diameter, an organ, a trombone, a cornet, three bugles, five violins, three World War I bayonets, and 10 clocks, including one 9 feet high and weighing 210 pounds). The rooms and hallways were honeycombed with tunnels through all this debris and booby-trapped so that anything disturbed would come crashing down on an intruder. The police began searching for the other brother, Langley, who had been caring for Homer, as it was thought that he might have phoned in the tip. After 8 weeks of burrowing through the incredible mess, they finally found the body of Langley Collyer wedged between a chest of drawers and a bedspring; he had been killed by one of his own booby traps.

For students writing literature reviews and research reports, the lesson of the Collyer brothers is that it is not always easy to discard things you have made an effort to save, including notes, studies, and quotes that you have taken trouble to track down. But quantity cannot replace quality and relevance in the material you save for your paper. Instructors are more impressed by tightly reasoned papers than by those that overflow with superfluous material. It is best to approach the writing and polishing stage with an open but focused mind, that is, a mind that is focused on the objective but is at the same time open to discarding irrelevant material (not research data, however).

The Self-Motivator Statement

To begin the first draft, write down somewhere for yourself the purpose or end goal you have in mind (that is, what your paper will be about). Keep this "self-motivator statement" brief so that you have a succinct focus for your thoughts as you enter them into your word processor or set them down on paper. You will be less apt to go off on a tangent if every once in a while you glance at this statement to remind yourself of your plan for the paper's direction.

We can imagine the following self-motivator statement that Jane Doe might have written as she began the first draft of her research report in appendix A:

Jane Doe's Motivator Statement

> I'm going to describe how I found that tipping increases when people are given a small gift, and how the manipulation of a reciprocity effect can further increase tipping. I will begin with a background review that puts my hypotheses in context, and I will conclude with some observations and ideas for further research.

And for John Smith, as he began the first draft of his review paper in appendix B, we can imagine the following motivator statement:

John Smith's Motivator Statement

> I'm going to compare the g-centered view of intelligence with what I am going to term the *multiplex view* because the way that different abilities are subsumed under the term *intelligence* reminds me of how different movies are housed together in a multiplex theater. I will emphasize Howard Gardner's theoretical approach, the criticisms, and the counterarguments. At the end, I will try to say something about both the current and the future directions of research in this area.

As you can see, this trick of using a self-motivator statement can help to concentrate your thoughts. It should also make the task of writing seem less formidable. Using the self-motivator is a good way simply to get you going and keep you clearheaded, and also to filter out material that can be discarded.

The Opening

A good opening is crucial to engaging the reader's attention and interest. Some writers are masters at creating good openings, but many technical articles and books in psychology start out ponderously. There are certainly enough cases of ponderous writing so that we need not give examples. But what about openings that grip our minds and make us want to delve further into the work?

One technique for beginning a paper in an inviting way is to pose a stimulating question. For example, psychologist Sissela Bok wrote a book about the ethics of lying, a subject many people would find pretty dry and uninviting, but she opened her book (*Lying: Moral Choice in Public and Private Life*, Pantheon, 1978) with a number of compelling questions that resonate with immediacy and vibrancy:

> Should physicians lie to dying patients so as to delay the fear and anxiety which the truth might bring them? Should professors exaggerate the excellence of their students on recommendations in order to give them a better chance in a tight job market? Should parents conceal from children the fact that they were adopted? Should social scientists send investigators masquerading as patients to physicians in order to learn about racial and sexual biases in diagnosis and treatment? Should government lawyers lie to Congressmen who might otherwise oppose a much-needed welfare bill? And should journalists lie to those from whom they seek information in order to expose corruption? (p. xv)

By posing these questions, Bok spoke to readers in the same way that she would if she were opening a dialogue. If we think about the questions, even for a moment, we are compelled to answer them, even if only subconsciously. We are drawn into the book because we want to compare Bok's answers to these questions with our own thinking (what psychologist Leon Festinger described as "social comparison").

Another technique is to try to rivet attention by impressing on readers the paradoxical nature of a timely issue. In *Obedience to Authority* (Harper, 1969), social psychologist Stanley Milgram began as follows:

> Obedience is as basic an element in the structure of social life as one can point to. Some system of authority is a requirement of all communal living, and it is only the man dwelling in isolation who is not forced to respond, through defiance or submission, to the commands of others. Obedience, as a determinant of behavior, is of particular relevance to our time. It has been reliably established that from 1933 to 1945 millions of innocent people were systematically slaughtered on command. Gas chambers were built, death camps were guarded, daily quotas of corpses were produced with the same efficiency as the manufacture of appliances. These inhumane policies may have originated in the mind of a single person, but they could only have been carried out on a massive scale if a very large number of people obeyed orders. (p. 1)

Milgram's passage first stirs our imagination because it reminds us that obedience is a basic part of social life. What ultimately draws us into Milgram's opening chapter is the matter-of-fact way that he refers to the grotesque nature of the Holocaust, letting the deadly facts speak for themselves.

This opening leads us to a conclusion, setting the stage for the rest of the book. Incidentally, this passage was written before there were concerns about sexist language: Milgram's use of the word *man* ("it is only the man dwelling in isolation") as a general term for men and women is now considered improper usage. Instead, he could have said "the person dwelling in isolation" (we return to this issue later).

However, perhaps you are thinking, "What does Milgram's or Bok's work have to do with me? These are noted Ph.D. psychologists who were writing books, but I'm just writing a paper for a course." The answer any instructor will give you is that an expectation of good writing that captures the reader's attention and draws the reader into the message is not limited to books or other published work. It also applies, for instance, to correspondence in businesses and organizations, company memos, and applications for jobs.

In the sample papers at the end of this book, what makes the opening passages inviting is that they also strike a resonant chord in the reader. Jane Doe's research report starts with interesting facts, which lead into the logic of her introduction and, ultimately, to her hypotheses. John Smith begins his review paper by referring to the elusive nature of *intelligence,* a term that is used in different ways. The concept of intelligence seemingly "cries out" for further clarification, and clarifying the term is what John proposes to do in the rest of his paper. In both introductions, there are smooth transitions into the following sections of the students' papers.

There are many useful opening techniques. You can start by defining the phenomenon of interest to you. Or you can describe a situation that the readers have probably experienced or will at least empathize with. Another trick is to start with an anecdote, like the one about the strange case of the Collyer brothers and how it is a metaphor for "pack rats." Some writers like to use an opening quotation, called an *epigraph,* to set the stage for what follows. All of these are devices that a writer can use to shape a beginning paragraph, or a first chapter of a thesis or dissertation. Not only should the opening lead the reader into the work, but at its best, it should provide momentum for the writer as the words begin to flow.

Settling Down to Write

Should you find yourself still having trouble beginning the introduction, try the trick of not starting with the introductory paragraph. Start writing whatever paragraph or section you feel will be the easiest, and then tackle the rest as your ideas begin to flow. When faced with a blank computer screen and a flashing cursor, some students escape by surfing the Net, playing video games, taking a nap, or wandering around to find somebody to chat with. Recognize these and similar counterproductive moves for what they are, because they can drain your energies. Use them instead as rewards *after* you have done a good job of writing.

The following are general pointers to ensure that your initial writing will go as smoothly as possible:

- While writing, try to work in a quiet, well-lighted place in 2-hour stretches (dim lighting makes people sleepy). Even if you are under time pressure to finish the paper quickly, it is important to take a break so you can collect your thoughts and make sure you are not writing aimlessly or drifting off in a wrong direction.
- When you take a break, go for a stroll, preferably outside, because the fresh air will be invigorating, and the change of environment will help you think about what you have already written and what you want to say next.
- If you are unexpectedly called away while you are in the middle of an idea, jot down a phrase or a few words that will get you back on track once you return to your writing. (Be sure to save your work before you leave.)
- When you stop for the day, try to stop at a point that is midway through a thought that you are finding difficult to express or complete. When you wake up the next day, your mind will be fresh with new ideas, and your writing will not have to start cold.
- Try to pace your work with time to spare so that you can complete the first draft and let it rest for a day. When you return to the completed first draft after a night's sleep, your critical powers will be enhanced, and you will have a fresh approach to shaping the final draft.

Ethics of Writing and Reporting

The most fundamental ethical principle in scholarly writing is honesty in all facets of the work. If you are doing empirical research and writing a report, this principle means honesty in all aspects of the project, from its implementation to your written account of the procedures that you used, your findings, their limitations, and their implications. Two examples of deliberate dishonesty are the falsification of data and the fabrication of results, which constitute fraud. Just as when the professional career of a scientist who falsifies data or fabricates results is compromised, the consequences will be harsh for the student writing a research report in which the data or results are fabricated. Claiming someone else's work as your work is another form of fabrication that will not be tolerated.

Knowingly misrepresenting the implications of actual findings is also unethical, whether it involves what Robert Rosenthal has called "hyperclaiming" (i.e., exaggerating the implications of research) or "causism" (i.e., falsely implying a causal relationship).[1] For example, using expressions such as "the effect of," "the impact of," "the consequence of," and "as a result of" clearly

---

[1]R. Rosenthal (1994). Science and ethics in conducting, analyzing, and reporting psychological research. *Psychological Science, 2,* 127–134.

implies that there is a causal relationship. But if the research design does not allow you to make a causal inference, you are guilty of hyperclaiming by using this language. To avoid this problem, simply use the appropriate language, expressions like "was related to," "was predictable from," or "could be inferred from." As Rosenthal argued, if the writer is aware of the problem, then falsely implying a causal relationship reflects blatant unethical misrepresentation and deception; on the other hand, the writer's lack of awareness reflects ignorance or lazy writing.

Honesty in research reporting and other scholarly writing also means giving credit where credit is due. For students, this means that if the instructor, a teaching assistant, or someone else helped you in some significant way, you acknowledge that contribution in an author note. The author notes of Jane Doe's and John Smith's papers illustrate this kind of acknowledgment.

Another important ethical imperative in science concerns the sharing of data with those who want to verify published claims by reanalyzing the results. Provided that the confidentiality of the study participants is protected, and unless legal rights preclude the release of the data, psychologists are expected to make their empirical findings available to other competent professionals. Although your paper is not a publication, instructors have the option to require students writing research reports to provide the raw data on which the work is based. If confidentiality is a potential problem, ask the instructor how the data might be coded to protect the privacy of those who have participated in your study.

Before we turn to what many instructors consider the most significant concern in student papers—the avoidance of plagiarism—we will mention one further standard with implications for students. It is unethical to misrepresent as fresh data any research results that have already been published or reported. If the data have been published or reported elsewhere, the researcher is expected to say so and to tell where. The purpose of this ethical rule is to avoid leading research consumers to mistakenly believe that a separate report of the same research findings implies that the research has been successfully replicated. For students who are writing research reports, this rule means that it is ethically unacceptable to submit the same work for additional credit in different courses. It may be acceptable to base the literature review in a research report for one course on the more extensive review in a paper for another course, but only with the full knowledge and consent of the instructors.

Avoiding Plagiarism

The nagging concerns of most instructors who teach writing-intensive courses are conveying the importance of originality and the meaning and consequences of plagiarism. The term *plagiarism,* which comes from a Latin word meaning "kidnapper," refers to the theft of another person's ideas or work and passing it off as one's own. It is crucial that you know what constitutes plagiarism and be aware that the penalties can be severe. Claiming not to know that you committed plagiarism is not an acceptable defense. Simply stated, taking someone else's work and passing it off as your own is wrong, and the penalty in a class assignment or a thesis will be severe.

In fact, it is quite easy to avoid committing plagiarism, even accidentally. All you must be is attentive and willing to make the effort to paraphrase the material in question (and to cite the source exactly), or else to quote the material word for word and put quotation marks around it (and, of course, cite the source and page number). If a passage you want to use is 40 or more words (as illustrated by the two passages that we quoted previously from Bok's and Milgram's books), then quotation marks are not used. Instead the passage is set off as a *block quotation*—indented about a half inch from the left margin, with the page number indicated in parentheses after the final period.

To illustrate plagiarism and how easily it can be avoided, assume that a student writing an essay came across Sissela Bok's book on lying and copied down the following passage for future reference:

> Deceit and violence—these are two forms of deliberate assault on human beings. Both can coerce people into acting against their will. Most harm that can befall victims through violence can come to them also through deceit. But deceit controls more subtly, for it works on belief as well as action. Even Othello, whom few would have dared to try to subdue by force, could be brought to destroy himself and Desdemona through falsehood. (Bok, 1978, p. 18)

There would be no problem if the student reproduced this passage just as it appears here, because the student has copied the passage accurately, has clearly indicated that it is quoted from Bok's work (by indenting the entire passage), and has properly noted the page on which it appeared. The plagiarism problem would arise if the student decided to change a word or two to make the passage sound a little different and then passed it off as an original thought. No need to mention Bok's book, the student thinks, because no one will bother to check, and even if the instructor should happen to recognize this passage, why, the student can plead "forgetting" to give Bok full credit. The student submits a paper containing the following passage incorporated into the narrative text (that is, it is not indicated as a quote with a few words changed):

> Deceit and violence are two forms of deliberate assault on human beings. Both can coerce people into acting against their will. Most harm that can happen to people through violence can also happen to them through deceit. However, deceit controls more subtly, because it works on belief as well as action. Even Othello, whom few would have dared to try to subdue by force, could be brought to destroy himself and Desdemona through falsehood.

Although it might sound like an A paper to the student, this passage, when seen in the context of the rest of the paper, will stick out like a sore thumb, and instructors are sensitive to inconsistencies like these. When the student is caught, the result will be an F in the course. Even if not caught red-handed, the student must nevertheless live with the knowledge of this deceit and the concern that this dishonesty may at some later point come back to haunt him or her.

Another word of caution: One instructor mentioned to us that, "although changing a word or two of an author's writing, failing to cite the source, and just passing it off as one's own work is certainly egregious, it is not the problem that many instructors run into more frequently." A more frequent problem, this instructor told us, is that students start off with something like "According to Bok (1978)," change some words, and simply repeat a passage without indicating that it is almost a word-for-word quote. Just changing a word or two in each sentence is not legal paraphrasing; it's plagiarism. The student needs to put the author's ideas into his or her own words and his or her own sentence structure.

Of course, if you believe that someone else has said something much better than you can ever hope to say it, quote (and cite) or paraphrase (and cite) the other source. For example, here is how the student might have incorporated Bok's ideas without falling into plagiarism:

> Bok (1978) made the case that deceit and violence "can coerce people into acting against their will" (p. 18). Deceit, she argued, controls more subtly because it affects belief. Using a literary analogy, Bok observed, "Even Othello, whom few would have dared to try to subdue by force, could be brought to destroy himself and Desdemona through falsehood" (p. 18).

Electronic plagiarizing is no more acceptable than plagiarizing from printed matter. If you find something on the Internet that you want to use, the same considerations of honesty apply. There is a specialized search engine that an instructor can use to look for stolen material or uncredited citations. The likelihood of not getting caught is diminishing rapidly. As mentioned before, it is a good idea to keep your notes, outlines, and rough drafts, because instructors will ask students for such material if a question arises about the originality of their work.

Lazy Writing

On hearing that quotations and citations are not construed by definition as plagiarism, some lazy students submit papers saturated with quoted material. Unless you feel it is absolutely essential, avoid quoting lengthy passages throughout a paper. What, then, would be appropriate occasions for quoting someone? If you are describing two competing views, for example, and want to be sure to represent both positions fairly, you may want to use direct quotations. Or someone's language may be so expressive and convincing that you believe quoting a portion of it will improve your presentation.

Thus, on some occasions, it may be advisable to quote something (with a citation, of course). However, quoting a statement that is not particularly momentous or poignant signals lazy writing. Your instructor expects your paper to reflect *your* thoughts after you have examined and synthesized material from sources you found pertinent. Lazy writing does not carry as severe a penalty as plagiarism, but it will mean a reduced grade in writing-intensive courses. The reason for a lowered grade is that lazy writing conveys the impression that the student has not put very much effort into the assignment. Furthermore, if you really cannot say something in your own words, your instructor will conclude that you do not understand it well enough to write about it.

Tone

As you write, keep in mind certain basic style points. The *tone* of your paper is the manner and attitude that are reflected in the way you express your ideas. Your writing should not sound arrogant or pompous, nor should it be either dull or flowery. How can you create an appropriate tone in a scholarly essay or research report in psychology? The answer is that it takes practice, and in the process of becoming skilled, you can learn by paying attention to how researchers and other academic scholars who communicate clearly and effectively express their ideas in an appropriate tone.

Here are some tips on how to create the right tone:

- Strive for an explicit, straightforward, interesting, but not emotional way of expressing your thoughts, findings, and conclusions (as illustrated in the sample papers).
- Try not to sound stilted or uncomfortably formal (instead of saying, "In the opinion of this writer," just state your opinion—period).
- Don't write in such a casual or informal way, however, that your paper reads like a letter to a favorite aunt ("Here's what Jones and Smith say" or "So I told the research participants").
- Try not to sound slick, like the glib reports on network TV and in supermarket tabloids.
- Strive for an objective, direct tone that keeps your reader subordinate to the material you are presenting. Instead of saying, "The reader will note that the results were . . . ," say, "The results were . . ."
- If your instructor finds it acceptable, don't be afraid to use the first person (but don't use it routinely throughout your paper), and don't refer to yourself as *we* unless you are clearly referring to a collaborative effort with someone else.
- Avoid wordiness. A famous writing manual is William Strunk, Jr., and E. B. White's *The Elements of Style.* One of Professor Strunk's admonitions is "Omit needless words. Omit needless words. Omit needless words."

Nonsexist Language

The question of *word gender* has become a matter of some sensitivity among many writers. One reason to discourage gender bias in written and spoken communication is that words can influence people's thoughts and deeds, and we do not want to reinforce stereotypes or prejudiced behaviors. However, there is sometimes a good reason not to use gender-free pronouns. Suppose a new drug has been tested only on male subjects. If the researchers used only gender-free pronouns when referring to their subjects, a reader might mistakenly infer that the results applied to both genders.

The point, of course, is to think before you write. In her book *The Elements of Nonsexist Usage* (Prentice Hall, 1990), Val Dumond made the following observation concerning overuse of the word *man:*

> When the word is used, that is the mental picture that is formed. The picture is what simultaneously represents a conceptual meaning to the interpreter. Since a female picture does not come to mind when the word *man* is used, it would follow that *man* does not represent in any way a female human. (p. 1)

When the issue of nonsexist language first gained prominence, writers used contrived words such as *s/he* and *he/she* to avoid sexist language. Not only are the forms *he/she* and *s/he* awkward, but if the actors in question are of one gender, the use of *he/she* or *s/he* would mislead the reader into thinking that the actors included both genders.

Another contrived practice is using the plural pronoun *they* as a singular pronoun to avoid the use of *he* to represent both genders. For example, it would be grammatically incorrect to write:

> When a *person* [singular] takes an idea from a published source, *they* [plural pronoun] must cite that source appropriately.

Because the subject (*person*) is singular, it is incorrect to use the plural pronoun *they*. One acceptable alternative is to write *she or he* rather than *they:*

> When a *person* takes an idea from a published source, *she or he* must cite that source appropriately.

A less wordy alternative is to make the entire sentence plural:

> When *people* take ideas from published sources, *they* must cite those sources appropriately.

In general, beware of masculine nouns and pronouns that will give a gender bias to your writing. There are two simple rules to keep in mind: First, use plural pronouns when you are referring to both genders, for instance, "They did . . ." instead of "He did . . ." and ". . . to them" instead of ". . . to him." Second, use masculine and feminine pronouns if the situation calls for them. For example, if the study you are discussing included only male subjects, the use of only masculine pronouns is appropriate.

Voice

The verb forms you use in your writing can speak with one of two voices: active or passive. You write in the *active voice* when you represent the subject of your sentence as performing the action expressed by your verb ("The study participant responded by . . ."). You write in the *passive voice* when the subject of your sentence undergoes the action expressed by your verb ("The response was made by the study participant . . .").

If you try to rely mainly on the active voice, you will have a more vital, compelling style:

Active Voice (Good)

Eleanor Gibson (1988) argued that perceptual development in humans is "an ever-spiraling path of discovery" (p. 37).

Passive Voice (Not as Good)

It was argued by Eleanor Gibson (1988) that perceptual development in humans is "an ever-spiraling path of discovery" (p. 37).

This quoted passage also illustrates when it is advisable to quote. The reason the writer chose this fragment is that it is especially expressive and eloquent, whereas trying to paraphrase it might not capture Gibson's idea with the same flair. Furthermore, quoting such an eminent authority as Eleanor Gibson lends weight to the writer's development of a particular argument.

Verb Tense

The verb tenses you use in your paper can get into a tangle unless you observe the following two basic rules: First, use the *past tense* to report studies that were done in the past ("Jones and Smith found . . ."). If you are writing a research report, both the method and the results sections can usually be written in the past tense because your study has already been accomplished ("In this study, data *were* collected . . ." and "In these questionnaires, there *were* . . ."). Second, use the *present tense* to define terms ("Multiplex, in this context, *means* . . ." and "A stereotype *is* defined as . . ."). The present tense is frequently used to make a general claim ("Winter days *are* shorter than summer days").

Some researchers save the *future tense* for the section of their research reports in which they discuss implications for further investigation ("Future research *will be* necessary . . ."). But it is not essential to use the future tense. Instead, you can use the present tense in this case to say, "Further investigation *is* warranted. . . ."

Notice that three spaced periods appear at the end of some of the examples above. These periods are called *ellipses* or *ellipsis points*, and they are used in these examples to indicate that the sentences continue. Although as a general rule ellipsis points are not used at the end of a quotation, we used them in these examples just to introduce you to this punctuation mark. Typically, ellipsis points are used somewhere in the middle of a lengthy quoted passage to indicate that selected words have been omitted.

Agreement of Subject and Verb

Each sentence in your paper must express a complete thought and have a *subject* (in general terms, something that performs the action) and a *verb* (an action that is performed or a state of being), as in the following:

> The study participants [subject] were [verb] introductory psychology students who were fulfilling a course requirement.

Because the subject is plural (*study participants*), the verb form used (*were*) is also plural. Thus, the verb and subject agree, a basic rule of grammar.

In most sentence forms, achieving this agreement is a simple matter, but trouble sometimes arises. For example, when you use *collective nouns* (those that name a group—for example, *committee, team, faculty*), they can be either singular or plural. When you think of the group as a single unit, use a singular verb ("The union *is* ready to settle"). Plurals are called for when you want to refer to the components of a group ("The faculty *were* divided on the issue").

Trouble may also pop up when words come between subject and verb, as in the following grammatically correct example:

> Therapy [singular subject], in combination with behavioral organic methods of weight gain, exemplifies [singular verb form] this approach.

Here, the subject is singular (*Therapy*) and therefore the verb that goes with that noun is also singular (*exemplifies*). It would be grammatically incorrect to write something like this, in which the subject is singular but the verb form is plural:

> Therapy, in combination with behavioral organic methods of weight gain, *exemplify* [plural verb form] this approach.

When using some words—such as *everyone* or *nobody*—students may be puzzled about whether to use a singular or plural verbal form. Use a *singular verb form* after the following: *each, either, everyone, someone, neither, nobody*. Here is a correct usage: "When everyone is ready, the experiment will begin."

Common Usage Errors

Confusing Homonyms

The inside front cover of this book lists pairs of words that are pronounced similarly (so they are called *homonyms*) and are therefore often confused with one another. Word-processing spelling checkers will not catch these errors. One instructor's recommendation was that students proofread their papers *aloud* before submitting them, and thus avoid the kind of skimming that misses usage errors.

One such pair of homonyms is *affect* and *effect,* which may still be readily confused even if you proofread the paper aloud. Here are several tips to help you sort out these two homonyms:

◆ In their most common form, *effect* is a noun meaning "outcome" (as in "Aggression is often an *effect* of frustration"), whereas *affect* is a verb meaning "to influence" (as in "The level of frustration *affects* how a person behaves").

◆ However, *effect* can also be used as a verb meaning "to bring about" (as in "The clinical intervention *effected* a measurable improvement").

◆ And *affect* can also be used as a noun meaning "emotion" (as in "Several of the patients participating in this clinical trial exhibited positive *affect*").

Incorrect Use of Singular and Plural

Another potential source of problems is the incorrect use of the singular and plural of some familiar terms. The following list shows the correct singular and plural forms:

Singular	*Plural*
analysis	analyses
anomaly	anomalies
appendix	appendixes or appendices (both are correct)
criterion	criteria
datum	data
hypothesis	hypotheses
phenomenon	phenomena
stimulus	stimuli

For example, one common usage error in student papers is the confusion of *phenomena* (plural term) with *phenomenon* (singular term). It would be incorrect to write, "This [singular pronoun] phenomena [plural subject] is [singular verb] of interest." The correct form is either "This phenomenon is . . ." (singular subject and singular verb) or "The phenomena are . . ." (plural subject and plural verb).

The word *data* can also be a source of confusion, and most grammarians feel that they have lost this battle. In *The New York Times* and most other mass media publications, *data* appears as both a singular and a plural noun. Strictly speaking, the word *data* is plural, and the word *datum* is singular, but *datum* has almost vanished from popular usage. Nonetheless, to use these words correctly in APA style, you would not write, "The data [plural subject] indicates [singular verb] . . ." or "The data shows . . ." Instead, you would write, "The data indicate . . ." or "The data show . . ."

Between and Among

In the past, another common source of confusion was in the use of the words *between* and *among*. We were taught to use *between* when referring to two items only, and to use *among* when there are more than two items. This distinction seems to be another that has gone out of style, however. For example, *Webster's* (the tenth edition as well as the eleventh edition) denies the correctness of the distinction of the words *between* and *within*. In the analysis of variance (abbreviated ANOVA), conventional usage is "between sum of squares" and "between mean square," even if the number of conditions being compared is more than two.

Prefixes

Other common problems concern the use of some *prefixes* in psychological terms:

- The prefix *inter-* means "between" (for example, *interpersonal* means "between persons"); the prefix *intra-* means "within" (for example, *intrapersonal* means "within the person").
- The prefix *intro-* means "inward" or "within"; the prefix *extra-* means "outside" or "beyond." The psychological term *introvert* thus refers to an "inner-directed personality"; the term *extravert* indicates an "outer-directed personality." (However, *The New York Times* and other mass media publications spell *extravert* as *extrovert,* which makes no sense.)
- The prefix *hyper-* means "too much"; the prefix *hypo-* means "too little." Hence, the term *hypothyroidism* refers to a deficiency of thyroid hormone. *Hyperthyroidism* denotes an excess of thyroid hormone, and a *hyperactive* child is one who is excessively active.

Participants Versus Subjects

Although not strictly a usage error, referring to human beings who participated in a study as *subjects* is no longer recommended by the APA. Although the term commonly appears in other than APA publications, the reasoning of those who object is that *subjects* sounds passive and nondescriptive, whereas human beings are active agents who initiate as well as react. The *APA Manual* recommends that writers use *participants* as a general term instead of *subjects,* but that writers also try to be more specific by using terms such as *respondents, children, patients, clients*—depending on the nature or role of those who took part in the study. However, many experimental psychologists still prefer the term *subjects,* and we use both terms (*subjects* and *participants*) in this manual.

Numerals

Another potential source of bafflement is the proper use of numerals in the APA style. In general, the APA recommends spelling out single-digit figures (*one, two, three, four, five, six, seven, eight, nine*) and using figures (*10, 20, 30, 40*) for numbers with more than one digit. However, there are exceptions to this rule. Here are seven APA rules to help you decide when to spell out numbers and when to use figures for numbers:

1. Although it is recommended that you not begin a sentence with a number, if you must do so, spell it out ("Twenty-nine students volunteered for this study" or "Fourteen percent of all the participants responded in the affirmative").
2. Numbers expressed as words in phrases and sentences should be spelled out (as in "two-tailed test" or the sentence "Only two of the participants refused to go further in the study").
3. Spell out *zero* and *one* when they are easier to understand than *0* and *1* ("zero-sum game" or "one-word response").
4. When single-digit numbers are part of a numerical group, use figures (for example, "5 of the 25 participants failed to answer this question").
5. Use figures for all numbers—even one-digit numbers—that immediately precede a unit of measurement (for example, 3 cm or 9 mg).
6. Use figures for units of age and time (4-year-old, 3 months, 2 days, 9 minutes), units of measurement (1 million, 3%), and numbers used in reference lists (pp. 4–6, 2nd ed., Vol. 4).
7. Use whatever is the universally accepted style for well-known expressions (the Ten Commandments).

Three additional APA rules for reporting singular and plural numbers, long sequences of numbers, and physical measurements are the following:

8. When reporting the plurals of numbers, add an *s* without an apostrophe. So the plural of *1990* is *1990s*, and the plural of *20* is *20s*.
9. Commas are used between groups of three digits (1,000,000), except for page numbers (page 1225), binary digits (001001), serial numbers (345789), degrees of freedom, and numbers to the right of a decimal point (2,300.1357).
10. When reporting physical units, use the metric system. For example, 1 foot is reported as .3048 m (or meter), and 1 inch becomes .0254 m. To avoid confusion, you might put a zero before the decimal (0.3048 m or 0.0254 m).

More on Punctuation

Periods

Besides the proper use of commas in reporting numbers, there are various other rules for the use of punctuation marks in your writing. Notice above that there was no period after the *m* symbol for "meter," because the APA style is not to use a period after a symbol, except when the symbol is at the end of a sentence (a *period* always ends a declarative sentence). Periods are, however, used following an abbreviation other than a physical unit, as in the following common abbreviations of Latin words:

cf.	from *confer* ("compare")
e.g.	from *exempli gratia* ("for example")
et al.	from *et alia* ("and others")
et seq.	from *et sequens* ("and following")
ibid.	from *ibidem* ("in the same place")
i.e.	from *id est* ("that is")
op. cit.	from *opere citato* ("in the work cited")
viz.	from *videlicet* ("namely")

If you continually write *eg.* or *et. al.* in your paper, you will be telling the instructor, "I don't know the meaning of these terms!" The reason is that *e.g.* is the abbreviation of two words, not one. Writing *eg.* announces that you believe (mistakenly) it is the abbreviation of one word. Putting a period after *et* tells the instructor that you believe (again, mistakenly) it is an abbreviation, which it is not; it is an entire Latin word.

With the exception of *et al.*, if you use any of these Latin abbreviations, the *APA Manual* recommends that you use them in parentheses and tabular material, and that you otherwise spell out these abbreviations. As an illustration, take the expression "for example"; in parentheses you would write it as "e.g." as in the following:

Herrnstein and Murray's (1994) book was widely debated (e.g., Andery & Serio, 1997; Andrews & Nelkin, 1996; Carroll, 1997).

Not in parentheses, spell the phrase out rather than abbreviate it:

Herrnstein and Murray's (1994) book was widely debated; see, for example, work by Andery and Serio (1997), Andrews and Nelkin (1996), and Carroll (1997).

Other abbreviations that are followed by a period are the short forms of English words, as illustrated by the following:

anon.	for *anonymous*
ch.	for *chapter*
diagr.	for *diagram*
ed.	for *editor* or *edition*
fig.	for *figure*
ms.	for *manuscript*
p.	for *page*
pp.	for *pages*
rev.	for *revised*

v.   for *versus* (in references to and text citations of court cases)

vol.   for *volume*

vs.   for *versus, against*

Another important APA rule is that, except for common abbreviations like those above, most abbreviations for terms are first spelled out for the reader. Suppose that you refer repeatedly to reaction time or an instrument called the Humboldt Upside-Down Test. You would write "reaction time (RT)" or the "Humboldt Upside-Down Test (HUDT)" at the first mention and then use the abbreviation RT or HUDT in the rest of your paper.

The APA's exception to this rule is that abbreviations listed as word entries in *Webster's Collegiate Dictionary* do not need to be defined first. For example, IQ, REM, AIDS, HIV, and ESP appear as words in *Webster's* and thus do not need to be defined or set off in parentheses the first time they are used in a psychology paper.

Commas and Semicolons

We have already covered the use of commas in numbers. Some other uses of the *comma* are the following:

1. Use commas to separate each of three or more items in a series ("Smith, Jones, or Brown"; "high, medium, and low scorers").
2. Use commas to set off introductory phrases in a sentence ("In another experiment performed 10 years later, the same researchers found . . .").
3. Use commas to set off thoughts or phrases that are incidental to, or that qualify, the basic idea of the sentence ("This variable, although not part of the researchers' main hypothesis, was also examined").
4. Put a comma before coordinating conjunctions (*and, but, or, nor, yet*) when they join independent clauses ("The subject lost weight, but he was still able to . . .").

A common error in student papers is to insert a comma before a transitional expression such as *however, moreover,* or *therefore* when it is used to connect two complete clauses in a compound sentence:

The participants voiced no concerns, however, it was quite obvious that they were uncomfortable.

To avoid making that grammatical mistake, you have several choices. One option is to use a *semicolon* (;) before *however,* instead of a comma:

The participants voiced no concerns; however, it was quite obvious that they were uncomfortable.

A second option for avoiding the misuse of the comma is to divide the compound sentence into two sentences:

> The participants voiced no concerns. However, it was quite obvious that they were uncomfortable.

A third option is to replace the transitional expression *however* with the conjunction *but,* preceded by a comma:

> The participants voiced no concerns, but it was quite obvious that they were uncomfortable.

As a general rule, a semicolon is called for when the thoughts in the two independent clauses are close, and the writer wishes to emphasize this closeness or to contrast the two thoughts. The following sentence is an example of the grammatically correct use of the semicolon to connect thoughts:

> Anorexia nervosa is a disorder whose victims literally starve themselves; despite their emaciated appearance, they consider themselves overweight.

In most instances, however, these longer sentences can be divided into shorter ones, which will be clearer:

> Anorexia nervosa is a disorder whose victims literally starve themselves. Despite their emaciated appearance, they consider themselves overweight.

The Colon

Generally, the *colon* (:) is used to indicate that a list will follow, or to introduce an amplification. The colon tells the reader, "Note what follows." Here is an example in which we see a colon used to indicate that a list follows:

> Subjects were given the following items: (a) four calling birds, (b) three French hens, (c) two turtle doves, . . .

An example of the amplification use of a colon is the title of John Smith's review paper in appendix B. Here is another example of amplification:

> Gardner (1983) postulated two forms of the personal intelligences: interpersonal and intrapersonal intelligence.

For another use of the colon, notice in the reference lists of the two sample papers that a colon is inserted between the place of publication of a book and the name of the publisher, for example, "Mahwah, NJ: Erlbaum" and "Englewood Cliffs, NJ: Prentice Hall" and "Cambridge, MA: Harvard University Press." We will have more to say about the punctuation used in references in the next chapter.

Punctuation in Quoted Passages

We mentioned ellipses (. . .) used in quoted passages to indicate that selected words have been intentionally omitted. You will sometimes also see in quoted passages brackets ([ ]) with words inside. The brackets tell us that the words are not part of the original quotation but were inserted by the writer who is using this quoted material. For example, omitting some words may make a quoted passage grammatically incorrect or may make something unclear, but either of these problems can be easily fixed by the insertion of a few connecting words in brackets.

Earlier, we also mentioned the importance of putting quotation marks around words that are quoted. An exception is a quotation of 40 or more words, in which case it is set off from the body of the text by means of indented margins, and quotation marks are omitted. However, if there is an internal quotation within the longer quotation, then *double quotation marks* (". . .") are inserted around the quote within a quote, as in the following example:

> What practical implications did Rosenthal and Jacobson (1968) draw from their research findings? They wrote:
>> As teacher-training institutions begin to teach the possibility that teachers' expectations of their pupils' performance may serve as self-fulfilling prophecies, there may be a new expectancy created. The new expectancy may be that children can learn more than had been believed possible, an expectation held by many educational theorists, though for quite different reasons. . . . The new expectancy, at the very least, will make it more difficult when they encounter the educationally disadvantaged for teachers to think, "Well, after all, what can you expect?" The man [*sic*] on the street may be permitted his opinions and prophecies of the unkempt children loitering in a dreary schoolyard. The teacher in the schoolroom may need to learn that those same prophecies within her [*sic*] may be fulfilled; she is no casual passer-by. Perhaps Pygmalion in the classroom is more her role. (pp. 181–182)

When a quoted passage is fewer than 40 words, double quotation marks are used, and the passage is simply inserted in the text as part of the narrative. If a smaller quote appears within the quoted passage, then *single quotation marks* ('. . .') are used to set off the quote within a quote, as in the following sentence:

> Participant B responded, "My feeling about this difficult situation was summed up in a nutshell by Jim when he said, 'It's a tough job, but somebody has to do it.'"

As this example also illustrates, if the appropriate punctuation is a period (as shown at the end of this sentence), it falls *within* the quotation marks. The same rule applies to a comma; it is inserted within the quotation marks. But if the appropriate punctuation is a colon or a semicolon, it is inserted *after* the closing quotation marks.

In the lengthy quote above, which begins, "As teacher-training institutions . . ." and ends ". . . in the classroom is more her role," notice that the numbers of the pages on which the passage appears in Rosenthal and Jacobson's book are shown in parentheses at the end. Notice also that the word *sic* (Latin, meaning "thus") is inserted in brackets in two places; it indicates that a word or phrase that appears strange or incorrect is quoted verbatim. If you wanted to make the point that a quoted passage ignores gender, you would insert in brackets the word *sic* as shown. But observe that we did not insert *sic* after every gender term. In the fourth sentence of the quotation, the masculine pronoun *his* was not set off by *sic* because the reference is "man on the street." In the fifth sentence, the feminine pronoun *she* is also not set off, because the referent is "within her."

Revising and Polishing

In the next chapter, we consider the details of producing the final draft of your paper. Revising and polishing the first draft are best done after you have been able to leave the manuscript entirely. When you approach your writing after having taken such a break (ideally, 24 hours or more), your critical powers will be sharper. Syntax errors, lapses in logic, and other problems will become evident, so that smoothing them out will be relatively simple.

As you reread and polish your writing, consider the following suggestions:

◆ Be concise.
◆ Break up long paragraphs containing a lot of disparate ideas into smaller, more coherent paragraphs.
◆ Be specific.
◆ Choose words for what they mean, not just for how they sound.
◆ Double-check punctuation.
◆ Don't use a long word when a short word will do.
◆ Don't be redundant (for example, "most unique" is redundant).
◆ Don't let spelling errors mar your writing.
◆ If you are unsure about how to spell a word, use the spelling checker on your word processor; if the answer you get seems ambiguous, check your dictionary.

Save and back up your work when you are ready to start composing and revising. Your word processing system will do this for you automatically at regular intervals, though you must specify the interval you want. You never know when the electricity will suddenly go out or someone will playfully or accidentally hit a wrong key, or you yourself might be distracted and hit a wrong key and send your latest work into oblivion.

Making a backup means not only storing something inside the computer's hard drive (that is, if it's *your* PC) but also copying it onto a floppy disk, ZIP disk, CD, or flash memory. Our habit is also to make a printout periodically. Having a printed copy will allow you to inspect and modify the layout to make sure it looks the way you want it to. It will also allow you to polish your writing in a format that is tangible, and the one that the instructor will be receiving. Sometimes spelling errors and murky passages that are less apparent on-screen jump out as your eye traverses a printed page.

8

Producing the Final Manuscript

This chapter provides you with guidelines and tips for producing a finished product. The layout and production of your final manuscript are like the icing on a cake. If the underlying structure is sound, the result will be smooth and predictable.

General Pointers

Writing on a computer means that the steps involved in first drafts, revisions, and final drafts are telescoped. The reason that these stages lose their formal definition is that the word-processing system allows you, with the stroke of a key or the click of a mouse, to shift or change words, sentences, paragraphs, and even entire sections as you compose and revise. In the old days, when students could use only a typewriter, it was painfully difficult to revise, because they had to equip themselves with scissors and glue to literally cut and paste and then each time had to retype those sections of the paper that had been changed. Of course, notes, long quotations, references, tables, and figures that you will need for your final draft can be easily stored in your computer's memory or on a disk or flash memory and can be retrieved as needed. The computer is not a substitute for the hard work of organizing your ideas, thinking them through, and expressing them clearly, but it releases you from an enormous amount of drudgery.

The spelling checkers and grammar checkers on word-processing systems are designed to flag mistakes, offer alternatives, and let you choose whether to make a particular change or to ignore the alternative recommendations. These programs are not infallible, so do not let them lull you into a false sense of security or into thinking that they are a substitute for careful proofreading of your final manuscript. Your spelling checker is based on a dictionary (actually a word inventory) in the word-processing system, and not all of the technical terms that psychologists and other professionals use are part of every word-processing inventory. If your spelling checker flags a word that you know is spelled correctly, click "Add," and the correct spelling will be added to the word inventory. Notice that there are lists of commonly misspelled words on the inside front and back covers of this manual; if you peruse this list once you have a draft of your proposal or final paper, some words may catch your eye as possible mistakes in your paper that the spelling checker missed.

Grammar checkers are designed to flag a sentence that violates a particular grammar or style rule. When it encounters what it has been programmed to define as a problem, a grammar dialogue box appears on the screen, and you are asked whether you want to accept a suggestion or ignore it. You can set up the word processor so that the grammar checker automatically searches for violations as you write and flags them as they are encountered, or you can simply turn off the grammar checker and use it only when you want it. As many experienced writers know, grammar checkers can be maddening because they often "catch" acceptable stylistic variations and fail to recognize stylistic requirements that may have been violated. Although it is essential to keep the spelling checker active, many writers (ourselves included) prefer not to use the grammar checker and instead depend on their own eyes and experience to catch mistakes and correct them.

Another tool in your word processor system is the thesaurus (or lexicon), which you access by clicking on the appropriate menu option. The thesaurus in your word processor system looks up synonyms for words or phrases, and you then choose whether to replace a word with one of the synonyms. You need to make sure that the replacement word means the same thing as your original word, a decision that only you can make. If you are not absolutely sure, look up the replacement word in your dictionary.

Here are more general pointers as you set about producing the final manuscript:

- ◆ Make sure the type is legible. If it is faint, invest in a new cartridge.
- ◆ Use double line spacing, and print on only one side of the sheet of paper, inserting a page header in the upper right corner and numbering pages as the two sample papers illustrate.
- ◆ Make a second copy of the finished paper. The original is for your instructor, and the duplicate copy will ensure the immediate availability of an exact spare copy in case of an unforeseen problem.
- ◆ Don't format your word processor to create a justified (even) right margin, which produces a block effect and, sometimes, odd spacing within lines. Instead, let the right margin remain ragged (uneven).
- ◆ Use a 12-point typeface, preferably Times New Roman or Courier, both of which are known as *serif* typefaces, so called because of the tiny line that finishes off the main strokes of a letter. If you are lettering drawings and figures, however, use a typeface without a serif (called *sans serif typefaces*) because it will provide a sharper visual presentation in graphics.
- ◆ Don't use the letter *l* to represent the numeral one or the letter *o* to represent a zero; instead use the separate 1 and 0 keys for

these digits. Also, don't use the letter *X* to represent chi; instead, insert the proper symbol (χ), which in Microsoft Word you will find in the "Symbol" submenu under "Insert" (or else write it in by hand).

◆ The *APA Manual* recommends the use of one space following all punctuation, including the space between sentences. However, if you are in the habit of inserting two spaces after a period (and some people are), do what is comfortable. (If you were submitting a copy manuscript to an APA journal, the manuscript would not be rejected on the basis of the spacing around punctuation.)

We turn now to other specifics of layout and processing that will help to give your finished paper a pleasing appearance.

Title Page Format

Glance at the title pages of the two sample papers at the end of this book. The title summarizes the main idea of the project and is centered near the top of the page. (Notice that the title appears again on page 3 of each sample paper.) A good title is succinct and yet adequately describes to the reader the gist of the work. If you arrived at a working title when narrowing your topic and drafting your proposal, that title can be changed or made more specific if you think it is no longer accurate or completely descriptive of the finished paper. (Incidentally, the *APA Manual* style is to capitalize prepositions of four or more letters in titles and headings, so you would capitalize *With* or *From*, for example, if it appears in the title of your paper.)

If you were producing a copy manuscript to be submitted to a journal, the *APA Manual* recommends that it resemble the sample title page in Exhibit 12. The title pages of Jane's and John's papers in appendixes A and B deviate from Exhibit 12 because their title pages are written for their instructors, and there is no need for a *running head* (the purpose of which is to suggest to a copyeditor an abbreviated title to be printed at the top of the pages of a published article), but the instructor has a good reason to ask for the other information on the students' title pages:

The page header and page number
The student's name (called the *byline*)
The student's e-mail address or other contact information
The number and name of the course or sequence for which the paper was written
The instructor's or adviser's name
The date the paper will be submitted

The page number in the upper-right corner is accompanied (on every page) by one or more words. These words are called *page headers,* and their purpose is to make it easy for the reader to identify each manuscript page if some pages become separated from the rest. It is easy to insert a page header

EXHIBIT 12   *Sample title page of copy manuscript in APA style*

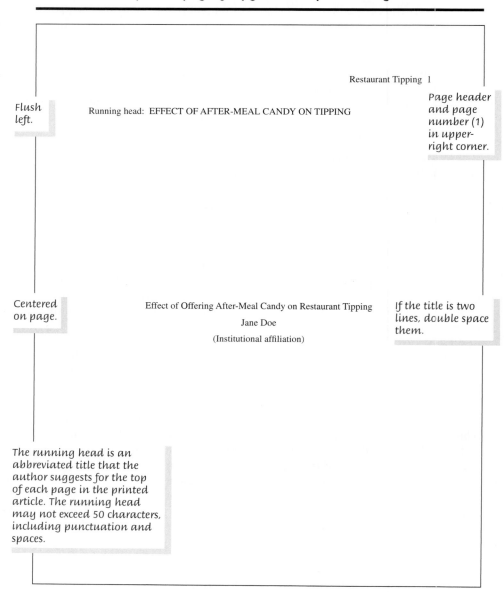

Restaurant Tipping 1

Flush left.

Running head: EFFECT OF AFTER-MEAL CANDY ON TIPPING

Page header and page number (1) in upper-right corner.

Centered on page.

Effect of Offering After-Meal Candy on Restaurant Tipping

Jane Doe

(Institutional affiliation)

If the title is two lines, double space them.

The running head is an abbreviated title that the author suggests for the top of each page in the printed article. The running head may not exceed 50 characters, including punctuation and spaces.

when using a word processor, and as you revise—cutting and pasting—the word processor will automatically update the page numbers.

Showing the instructor's name (if the paper is submitted for a course) or the adviser's name (if the paper is submitted to fulfill some other requirement, such as a "prelim" paper) is a courtesy. If the paper is a thesis, another courtesy is to include an acknowledgment page (after the title page) on which you thank your adviser and any others who extended a helping hand as you worked on your project. Incidentally, theses also usually include a table of contents page.

Headings

It is customary to break up the text of a lengthy paper with brief but informative headings. One purpose of these headings is to provide a conceptual map that enables readers to understand exactly where they are as they examine the sequence of topics or issues discussed in the paper. Another purpose is to organize the writer's thinking, so that topics that belong in one section do not accidentally stray into another section where they do not belong. A third purpose is to shepherd readers through the logical flow of the paper, from the most important to the least important (but still relevant) topics, issues, or information.

If you are writing a review paper, thesis, or some other kind of term paper, you should be able to derive these headings from the outline of your paper or thesis. Observe, for example, how John Smith's headings and subheadings lend symmetry to his review paper, showing its progressive development in concise phrases. John's paper uses two formats of headings: center and flush left. *Center headings* are used to separate the paper into major sections, are written in uppercase and lowercase letters, and are not italicized:

Two Issues in Intelligence Testing
The Traditional Theoretical Orientation
The Multiplex Theoretical Orientation
Gardner's Idea of Multiple Intelligences
Some Criticisms and Rejoinders
Conclusions

To subdivide these major sections, John uses *subheadings* that are flush left, in italics, and in uppercase and lowercase. John uses three subheadings to partition the major section labeled "Gardner's Idea of Multiple Intelligences":

Eight Criteria of Intellectual Talents
Seven Types of Intelligence
Independence of Abilities

If John had needed to use a second level of subheadings, they would be indented and italicized, the first word in each subheading would be capitalized and other words in lowercase, the subheading would end with a period, and the body of the text would follow it immediately. For example, the second level of subheadings might look like the following had John wanted to partition the section labeled *"Seven Types of Intelligence"* and begun with a *"People to be studied"* subheading:

Seven Types of Intelligence

People to be studied. Using the eight criteria above as a base, Gardner argued the importance of studying people within the "normal" range of intelligence, and also of studying those who are gifted or expert in various domains valued by different cultures (Gardner, 1993a). He further emphasized the importance of studying people who have suffered selective brain injuries. Drawing on the eight criteria above . . .

If you are writing a research report, you use section headings and first-level subheadings that are inherent in the structure of most research reports in psychology when only a single study or experiment is reported. In Jane Doe's research report, under the major heading of "Method," she uses three subheadings:

Method

Participants
Materials
Design and Procedure

In the "Results" section, Jane uses not only first-level subheadings, but second-level subheadings as well, which are indented, italicized, first word capitalized and other words in lowercase, and followed by a period, with the body of the text immediately following the subheading:

Overall Findings

Basic data. Table 1 (which appears on the next to last page of this report) shows the average tip percentages in the four conditions, that is, the means (M) of the columns of values shown in the appendix. As predicted, the mean tip percentage increased from . . .

Further levels of subheadings are used by writers preparing more lengthy or complex manuscripts, but the ones illustrated here should suffice for students writing review papers and research reports.

Italicizing

Before the days of word processors, underlining was used to indicate to typesetters that selected text was to be set in italics. Nowadays, of course, it is a simple matter to format text in italics. The APA does not object, however, if authors of manuscripts submitted for publication use underlining rather than italics, because once a copy manuscript is accepted for publication, copyeditors who work with hard copy manuscripts will insert an underline anyway (to indicate italics to the printer). Conventional usage also calls for the titles of books mentioned in the body of the text to be italicized. For example, John Smith writes, "Herrnstein and Murray (1994), in a book entitled *The Bell Curve,* ignited a spirited debate about . . ."

Italicizing is also used in other ways; the following are the *APA Manual*'s guidelines for these other uses:

- Letters used as statistical symbols are italicized: *F, N, n, P, p, t, z,* and so forth. Note that some symbols are in lowercase, and this can be very important. For example, an uppercase *N* indicates the total number of sampling units, and a lowercase *n* indicates the number of units in a subsample of *N.*
- Greek letters used as statistical symbols are not italicized, for example, the symbol for chi-square (χ^2), the symbol instructing us to sum a set of scores (Σ), the symbol for the standard deviation of a population of scores (σ), and the symbol for the variance of a population of scores (σ^2).
- In reference lists, volume numbers of journal articles and titles of books and journals are italicized.
- Words that you wish to emphasize are italicized, but use this device sparingly ("Effective teaching, the authors asserted, will come only from the teachers' firm belief that their pupils *can* perform").
- Words used to illustrate are italicized ("the term *knowing . . .*" or ". . . is called *knowing*"). John Smith writes, "Some people are referred to as *street smart,* a term implying that they are intellectually shrewd in the ways of the world," and "In sum, whether psychological and educational researchers mean by *intelligence* (a) the ability to adapt to the environment, (b) the ability . . ."

If you need to insert in a paper a statistical formula with superscripts and subscripts, your word processor may have simple formulas you can access. We used an equation-editing program (*MathType*) to insert formulas in the appendix of Jane Doe's research report. Using an equation-editing program gives the writer the option of italicizing the units of a formula, but most instructors will be happy if the student writes any needed formulas by hand.

Citations in Text

There are several simple conventions for citing an author's work in the narrative text of a paper. The purpose of a citation is to make it easy for the reader to identify the source of a quotation or an idea and then to locate the particular reference in the list at the end of the paper. The author-date method is the format stipulated in the *APA Manual.* The surname of the author and the year of publication are inserted in the text at the appropriate point.

One APA rule is not to list any publication in your reference list that you do not cite. The exception would be if you were developing an extensive bibliography for a dissertation or a thesis and wanted to list every relevant article and book on the subject, whether you discussed them in your manuscript or not. However, you will not be expected to compile such a bibliography for a review paper or a research report in a course.

Another APA rule is not to cite any source material in the text without placing it in the list of references. The exception to this rule is a personal communication that you cite in the text, because it is unnecessary to put it in the list of references as well. An example can be found in the author note of John Smith's review paper, where he thanks Professor Robert Rosenthal for permission to reproduce a graphic, and John notes, "(personal communication, April 10, 2007)." Another way of citing this communication is "(R. Rosenthal, personal communication, April 10, 2007)."

Numerous examples of citations occur in the two sample papers, and here are some more examples of how reference materials are cited in APA style. Notice below that the word *and* is spelled out in the narrative citation of "Stella, Doyle, *and* Hooper," but an ampersand (&) is used in the parenthetical citation:

Citation in Narrative ("and")

Stella, Doyle, and Hooper (2006) investigated whether having children listen to Mozart was correlated with improved attention span in the classroom.

Citation in Parentheses ("&")

The correlation between listening to Mozart and improved attention span in the classroom was investigated in young children (Stella, Doyle, & Hooper, 2006).

These examples also illustrate the convention of author-date citations that dictates the listing of the surnames of up to five authors the first time the citation is given. In any subsequent citations, if there are more than two authors, give the surname of only the first author, followed by *et al.* (not italicized) and the date:

Subsequent Citation (Use of "et al.")

Stella et al. (2006) also explained why they had expected a positive correlation between listening to Mozart and improved attention span in the classroom.

To cite a source that you did not read in its original form, make it clear that you are using someone else's citation (called a *secondary citation*). Use a secondary source only if the original source is unavailable to you; otherwise examine and cite the original source yourself. The reason to refrain from using secondary sources is that there is no guarantee that the material you want to cite is described correctly in the secondary source. However, as one instructor recently reminded us, community college libraries and other small libraries may not provide direct access to all of the primary sources needed by students.

Here are two examples of secondary citations. The first shows the secondary citation of a classic work, and the second shows two different citations of two secondary sources in the same sentence:

Secondary Citation of a Classic Work

In Virgil's epic poem, *The Aeneid* (as cited in Allport and Postman, 1947), the following characterization of Fama appears: . . .

Two Secondary Citations in the Same Sentence

Hasher, Goldstein, and Toppino's finding (as cited in Kendzierski & Markey, 2002) is also consistent with the traditional idea that merely being exposed over and over to the same message, even if it is blatantly false, is usually enough to instill confidence in its credibility (McCullough, Murphy, & Schwartz, 1911, as cited in Baldwin & Baldwin, 2004).

To cite a specific document obtained from a Web site, use a format similar to that for printed material (as shown above). If all you want is to cite a particular Web site but not a specific document from a Web site, give the address of the site but do not include it in your references section:

Web Site Citation

Easy-to-use templates that you fill in with reference information to see how a citation or reference should appear in APA style are available on David Warlick's Citation Machine Web site (http://citationmachine.net/index.php?source=58&callstyle=2&all=#here).

Here are some additional APA guidelines that will cover most of the cases that you are likely to encounter:

- ◆ If you are citing a series of works, the proper sequence is alphabetical order by the surname of the first author and then by chronological order. If the surnames are the same for two authors, then the citation is alphabetized by the first name (M. Baenninger, 2007; R. Baenninger, 2007; Brecher, 2002; DiClemente, 2000; DiFonzo & Bordia, 1993; Esposito, 2006; Frei, 2002; Kimmel, 2004; Strohmetz, 2001; Wells & Lafleur, 1999).
- ◆ Two or more works published by the same author in the same year are designated as *a, b, c,* and so on (Hantula, 2002a, 2002b, 2002c). In the references section, the alphabetical order of the works' titles determines the sequence when there is more than one work by an author in the same year.

◆ Work accepted for publication but not yet printed is designated *in press* (Stern, in press; Trimble, in press). In a list of citations of work by the same author, the rule is to place this work last: (Foster, 2003, 2005, in press). In other words, three works by Foster are cited, one published in 2003, the second in 2005, and the third accepted but not yet published.

If you run into a problem that these guidelines do not address, check out David Warlick's Citation Machine Web site (cited above). But even the APA is flexible, and journal editors will not return manuscripts just because the format of one unusual citation deviates from the APA norm. Once a copy manuscript is accepted for publication, corrections are made during the copy-editing process. Therefore, keep one general idea in mind as you go beyond these specific guidelines: If you run into a problem, ask yourself whether you could identify a reference based on the citation you have provided. In other words, put yourself in your reader's shoes, but also try to be consistent.

Tables and Figures

As discussed earlier in this book, tables and figures can be used to augment the presentation of the results. Often, however, when students include tables in their research reports, they are merely presenting their raw data in a neat format. Save your raw data for the appendix of your report (if your raw data are required), as shown in Jane Doe's report. Keep in mind that statistical tables in results sections of research reports are intended to *summarize* the raw data.

The *APA Manual* stipulates that tables and figures, numbered in the order in which they are first mentioned in the narrative, be put on separate pages at the end of the copy manuscript. Notice that the titles of the tables in Jane's report appear above the tables. If these were figures, the title (called the *caption*) would appear below the figure in the printed article, and the word *Figure* and the number of the figure would be in italics. When a copy manuscript is submitted to an APA journal, the figure captions are placed on separate pages, preceding the pages that refer to the figures. These requirements can get confusing for students who are producing final manuscripts for a course. The convention we use in this manual is to place the caption below the figure (as shown in John's Figure 1 in appendix B).

If you are using tables, notice that Jane's table titles, in uppercase and lowercase letters, are flush left and italicized. Each column of a table is expected to have a heading, including the left-most column (called the *stub column*). Column headings identify the items below them, and some tables use a hierarchy of headings (known as *decked heads*) to avoid repeating words. When the top heading in the hierarchy spans the body of the table, it is called a *table spanner*. But these are technical details. Just remember to keep your table headings clear, concise, and informative, so the reader can easily understand what is in the table.

If you are confused about the difference between a table and a figure, think of figures as bar graphs and line graphs. Graphics that are photographed or imported from artwork are also considered figures. As we mentioned earlier, because figures can introduce distortions that detract from a clear, concise summary of the data, most researchers prefer to use tables when giving precise summary details (group means and standard deviations, for example). If you must use a figure, do not overcomplicate it so that it is tedious to comprehend. The basic rule is to use only figures that add to the text and not to repeat what you can say very clearly in words. (If you are interested in learning about the psychology and art of graphic design, see the recommended readings at the end of chapter 6.)

If you need to add some clarifying or explanatory information to a table, it is customary to place this information below the table, as illustrated in Jane's report. The word *Note* is in italics with a period, and the information follows. To add a few specific notes to a table, the convention is to use superscript lowercase letters (^{a} ^{b} ^{c}) or asterisks (* ** ***). The following cases illustrate this usage:

Superscript Notation

$^a n = 50$ $\qquad$ $^b n = 62$

Asterisk Notation

$^* p < .05$ $\qquad$ $^{**} p < .01$ $\qquad$ $^{***} p < .0005$

List of References

The list of references starts on a new page, with the title "References" centered at the top of the page. The references are arranged alphabetically by the surname of the first author and then by the date of publication. Prefixes (*von, Mc, Mac, de, du*) can give students pause as they try to figure out how to alphabetize them, and the *APA Manual* has specific rules based on whether or not the prefix is customarily used when the person is referred to. Rather than wrestle with these nuances, just alphabetize by the article or preposition when you add such names to your list of references.

The standard style guidelines in the *APA Manual* are as follows:

- ◆ Invert all authors' names (that is, last name, first initial, middle initial).
- ◆ List authors' names in the exact order in which they appear on the title page of the publication.
- ◆ Use commas to separate authors and an ampersand (&) before the last author.
- ◆ Give the year the work was copyrighted (the year and month for magazine articles and the year, month, and day for newspaper articles).

◆ In titles of books, chapters in books, and journal articles, capitalize only the first word of the title and of the subtitle (if any) as well as any proper names.
◆ Give the issue number of the journal in parentheses if the article cited is paginated by issue.
◆ Italicize the volume number of a journal article and the title of a book or a journal.
◆ Give the city and state of a book's publisher, using the postal abbreviations listed in Exhibit 13. Major cities in the United States (such as Baltimore, Boston, Chicago, Dallas, Los Angeles,

EXHIBIT 13 **Postal abbreviations for states and territories**

Location	Abbreviation	Location	Abbreviation
Alabama	AL	Montana	MT
Alaska	AK	Nebraska	NE
Arizona	AZ	Nevada	NV
Arkansas	AR	New Hampshire	NH
California	CA	New Jersey	NJ
Colorado	CO	New Mexico	NM
Connecticut	CT	New York	NY
Delaware	DE	North Carolina	NC
District of Columbia	DC	North Dakota	ND
Florida	FL	Ohio	OH
Georgia	GA	Oklahoma	OK
Guam	GU	Oregon	OR
Hawaii	HI	Pennsylvania	PA
Idaho	ID	Puerto Rico	PR
Illinois	IL	Rhode Island	RI
Indiana	IN	South Carolina	SC
Iowa	IA	South Dakota	SD
Kansas	KS	Tennessee	TN
Kentucky	KY	Texas	TX
Louisiana	LA	Utah	UT
Maine	ME	Vermont	VT
Maryland	MD	Virginia	VA
Massachusetts	MA	Virgin Islands	VI
Michigan	MI	Washington	WA
Minnesota	MN	West Virginia	WV
Mississippi	MS	Wisconsin	WI
Missouri	MO	Wyoming	WY

New York, Philadelphia, and San Francisco) can be listed without a state abbreviation.

◆ If you are listing a foreign city other than Amsterdam, Jerusalem, London, Milan, Moscow, New Delhi, Paris, Rome, Stockholm, Tokyo, or Vienna, then use the country name as well.

Using these guidelines and the notes and examples shown below, you should encounter few problems. If you experience a problem, remember there is David Warlick's Citation Machine (cited before) and the APA *Publication Manual* Web site (http://www.apastyle.org). Remember, too, that the APA's rule of thumb in all cases is to be clear, consistent, and complete in referencing source material. Exhibit 14 has a summary list of the numbered examples that are shown below:

Authored Book

1. Single author
Invert the author's name, using initials for the first and middle names, and give the year of publication, the italicized title of the book (capitalizing the first word of the title and subtitle), and the location and name of the publisher in its shortened form.

> Kimmel, A. J. (1996). *Ethical issues in behavioral research: A survey.* Cambridge, MA: Blackwell.

2. More than one author
The style is the same as in the above reference, but insert a comma followed by an ampersand (&) before the last author's name.

> Shadish, W. R., Cook, T. D., & Campbell, D. T. (2001). *Experimental and quasi-experimental designs for generalized causal inference.* Boston: Houghton Mifflin.

3. Institutional author and publisher are the same
Give the full name of the institution, and list the publisher's name as "Author" when it is the same as the institutional author.

> American Psychiatric Association. (1994). *Diagnostic and statistical manual of mental disorders* (4th ed.). Washington, DC: Author.

Work in Press

4. Edited volume in production but not yet published
An edited volume or book that has been accepted by the publisher and is presumed to be in the process of production is considered "in press." Insert in parentheses the abbreviation "Ed." (if one editor) or "Eds." (if more than one editor), followed by a period, and then write "in press" in parentheses, followed by a period.

> Nezu, A. M., & Nezu, C. M. (Eds.). (in press). *Evidence-based outcome research: A practical guide to conducting randomized controlled trials for psychosocial interventions.* New York: Oxford University Press.

EXHIBIT 14 References illustrated in this chapter

Authored Book
1. *Single author*
2. *More than one author*
3. *Institutional author and publisher are the same*

Work in Press
4. *Edited volume in production but not yet published*
5. *Journal article accepted for publication but not yet in print*
6. *Chapter in edited book in production but not yet in print*
7. *Authored book in production but not yet in print*
8. *Monograph in a journal issue not yet in print*

Edited Published Work
9. *Single editor of a book*
10. *More than one editor, more than one volume, revised edition*

Work Republished at a Later Date
11. *Book of collected work*
12. *Single volume in multivolume series of collected work*
13. *Chapter in an anthology*

Article or Chapter
14. *Article by a single author in journal paginated by volume*
15. *Article by up to six authors in journal paginated by volume*
16. *More than six authors*
17. *Chapter in edited book*
18. *Chapter author with hyphenated first and last names*
19. *Entry in encyclopedia paginated by volume*
20. *Article in newsletter paginated by issue*
21. *Article in journal paginated by issue*

Non-English Publication
22. *Book*
23. *Journal article*

5. Journal article accepted for publication but not yet in print
A manuscript that has been officially accepted for publication by the editor of a journal is considered "in press," not merely a manuscript that has been submitted to a journal.

> Frei, R. L., Racicot, B., & Travagline, A. (in press). The impact of monochromic and type A behavior patterns on faculty research productivity and job-induced stress. *Journal of Managerial Psychology.*

EXHIBIT 14 Continued

Chapter in Multivolume Edited Series
  24. *Different author and editor*
  25. *Same author and editor*
Mass Media Article
  26. *Magazine article*
  27. *Newspaper article (author listed)*
  28. *Newspaper article (no author listed)*
Dictionary or Encyclopedia
  29. *Dictionary (no author listed)*
  30. *Encyclopedia (more than one volume, two publishers in two locations)*
Doctoral Dissertation or Master's Thesis
  31. *Doctoral dissertation abstract*
  32. *Unpublished doctoral dissertation*
  33. *Master's thesis (outside the United States)*
Unpublished Material
  34. *Technical report*
  35. *Unpublished manuscript*
  36. *Manuscript submitted for publication (but not yet accepted)*
  37. *Paper (unpublished) presented at a meeting*
  38. *Poster presented at a meeting*
Audiovisual Media
  39. *Motion picture*
  40. *Television broadcast*
  41. *Music recording*
Electronic Resources
  42. *Abstract retrieved from PsycINFO*
  43. *Full-text article retrieved from PsycARTICLES*
  44. *Same article retrieved electronically (another option)*
  45. *Article in Internet-only journal*
  46. *Information retrieved from Web site*

6. Chapter in edited book in production but not yet in print
A chapter that has been accepted by the editor of a book that, in turn, has been accepted by the publisher is considered "in press." Notice that the editors' names are not inverted, whereas the chapter authors' names are inverted as usual.

> Suls, J., & Martin, R. (in press). Social comparison processes in the physical health domain. In A. Baum, T. Revenson, & J. Singer (Eds.), *Handbook of health and psychology.* Mahwah, NJ: Erlbaum.

7. Authored book in production but not yet in print

A book manuscript that has been accepted by the publisher and is in the process of being prepared for publication is considered "in press." Notice that the state as well as the city is listed in this illustration, the reason being that there is also a Cambridge in the United Kingdom.

> Fine, G. A. (in press). *Mushroom worlds: Naturework and the taming of the wild*. Cambridge, MA: Harvard University Press.

8. Monograph in a journal issue not yet in print

A monograph is a lengthy manuscript that the journal publishes either separately as a supplement or as a whole issue of the journal. This example refers to a monograph accepted by the editor but not yet printed; once the monograph is published, the issue number and the supplement or part number (if it is published separately) are indicated in parentheses after the volume number.

> Lana, R. E. (in press). Choice and chance in the formation of society. *Journal of Mind and Behavior.*

Edited Published Work

9. Single editor of a book

After the editor's name, insert "Ed." in parentheses, followed by a period, the italicized title of the book, and so forth.

> Morawski, J. G. (Ed.). (1988). *The rise of experimentation in American psychology.* New Haven, CT: Yale University Press.

10. More than one editor, more than one volume, revised edition

To indicate more than one editor, "Eds." is inserted in parentheses, followed by a period. The number of the edition and the number of volumes (and the abbreviation "Vols.," capitalized) are noted in parentheses after the title. If this were the first revised edition, the abbreviation "Rev. ed." can be substituted for "2nd ed."

> Gilbert, D. T., Fiske, S. T., & Lindzey, G. (Eds.). (1988). *The handbook of social psychology* (4th ed., Vols. 1–2). Boston: McGraw-Hill.

Work Republished at a Later Date

11. Book of collected work

The date that the original work appeared is included in parentheses after the full citation of the current edition.

> Demosthenes. (1852). *The Olynthiac and other public orations of Demosthenes.* London: Henry G. Bohn. (Original work written 349 B.C.)

12. Single volume in multivolume series of collected work

The years in parentheses (1779/1971) indicate that the original work was published in 1779 and the current edition in 1971; the number of the particular volume in which the work appears is indicated in parentheses after the title of the series.

> Lessing, G. E. (1779/1971). *Gotthold Ephraim Lessing: Werke* (Vol. 2). München, Germany: Carl Hanser Verlag.

13. Chapter in an anthology

The years in parentheses (1733/1903) indicate the date of publication of the original work and the anthology. The pages on which the work appears in the anthology are indicated in parentheses after the title of the anthology, followed by a period.

> Pope, A. (1733/1903). Moral essays: Epistle I. To Sir Richard Temple, Lord Cobham, of the knowledge and character of men. In H. W. Boynton (Ed.), *The complete poetical works of Pope* (pp. 157–160). Boston: Houghton Mifflin.

Article or Chapter

14. Article by a single author in journal paginated by volume

The journal name and volume (*42*) are written in italics, followed by the page numbers (97–108, not in italics) of the article.

> Scott-Jones, D. (1994). Ethical issues in reporting and referring in research with low-income minority children. *Ethics and Behavior, 42,* 97–108.

15. Article by up to six authors in journal paginated by volume

An ampersand (&) is placed before the last author's name, and only the journal name and volume are italicized.

> Gabrieli, J. D. E., Fleischman, D. A., Keane, M. M., Reminger, S. L., & Morrell, F. (1995). Double dissociation between memory systems underlying explicit and implicit memory in the human brain. *Psychological Science, 6,* 76–82.

16. More than six authors

If there are seven or more authors, only the first six are listed, followed by a comma and "et al." (no ampersand).

> Thomas, C. B., Hall, J. A., Miller, F. D., Dewhirst, J. R., Fine, G. A., Taylor, M., et al. (1979). Evaluation apprehension, social desirability, and the interpretation of test correlations. *Social Behavior and Personality, 7,* 193–197.

17. Chapter in edited book

The authors' names are inverted, but not the editors' names. The page numbers of the chapter (pp. 130–165) are placed in parentheses immediately after the italicized title of the book, followed by a period.

> Aditya, R. N., House, R. J., & Kerr, S. (2000). Theory and practice of leadership: Into the new millennium. In C. L. Cooper & E. A. Locke (Eds.), *Industrial and organizational psychology: Linking theory and practice* (pp. 130–165). Cambridge, MA: Blackwell.

18. Chapter author with hyphenated first and last names

Hyphens in the first name and last name are retained, with all other information presented as before.

> Perret-Clermont, A.-N., Perret, J.-F., & Bell, N. (1991). The social construction of meaning and cognitive ability in elementary school children. In L. Resnick, J. M. Levine, & S. B. Teasley (Eds.), *Perspectives on socially shared cognition* (pp. 41–62). Washington, DC: American Psychological Association.

19. Entry in encyclopedia paginated by volume

The volume and page numbers of the entry are indicated in parentheses after the italicized title of the encyclopedia. Unusual in this example is that there were two publishers of the encyclopedia, both (as indicated) located in the same city.

> Stanley, J. C. (1971). Design of controlled experiments in education. In L. C. Deighton (Ed.), *The encyclopedia of education* (Vol. 3, pp. 474–483). New York: Macmillan & Free Press.

20. Article in newsletter paginated by issue

Immediately after the italicized volume number (*23*), the issue number is indicated (4, no italics) in parentheses.

> Camara, W. J. (2001). Do accommodations improve or hinder psychometric qualities of assessment? *The Score Newsletter, 23*(4), 4–6.

21. Article in journal paginated by issue

The format is the same as the one above.

> Valdiserri, R. O., Tama, G. M., & Ho, M. (1988). The role of community advisory committees in clinical trials of anti-HIV agents. *IRB: A Review of Human Subjects Research, 10*(4), 5–7.

Non-English Publication

22. Book

Diacritical marks (an umlaut in *Störeffekte* in this example) and capital letters are used for non-English words in the same way they were used in the original language. The English translation of the book's title is included in brackets immediately after the non-English title, followed by a period.

> Gniech, G. (1976). *Störeffekte in psychologischen Experimenten* [Artifacts in psychological experiments]. Stuttgart, Germany: Verlag W. Kohlhammer.

23. Journal article
The same rule referring to the use of diacritical marks and capital letters applies to the non-English title of the article and the name of the journal (however, the name of the journal is not translated into English).

> Foa, U. G. (1966). Le nombre huit dans la socialization de l'enfant [The number eight in the socialization of the infant]. *Bulletin du Centre d'Études et Recherches Psychologiques, 15,* 39–47.

Chapter in Multivolume Edited Series

24. Different author and editor
Volume and page numbers of the chapter are indicated in parentheses after the italicized series title.

> Kipnis, D. (1984). The use of power in organizations and interpersonal settings. In S. Oskamp (Ed.), *Applied social psychology* (Vol. 5, pp. 171–210). Newbury Park, CA: Sage.

25. Same author and editor
Notice that the chapter author's name is inverted, but the same name is not inverted when the author is also the editor of the series in which the chapter appears.

> Koch, S. (1959). General introduction to the series. In S. Koch (Ed.), *Psychology: A study of a science* (Vol. 1, pp. 1–18). New York: McGraw-Hill.

Mass Media Article

26. Magazine article
In parentheses followed by a period, the year and month(s) (if published monthly) and the day (if published more frequently than monthly) are indicated. If the volume number is known, then it is indicated as shown here in italics (*29*), followed by the page numbers.

> Csikszentmihalyi, M. (1996, July/August). The creative personality. *Psychology Today, 29,* 36–40.

27. Newspaper article (author listed)
All the page numbers are indicated for an article that appears on discontinuous pages, and the page numbers are separated by a comma.

Grady, D. (1999, October 11). Too much of a good thing? Doctor challenges drug manual. *The New York Times,* Section F, pp. 1, 2.

28. Newspaper article (no author listed)

When no author's name is listed in a newspaper article, the work is referenced by the title of the article and alphabetized in the list of references by the first significant word in the title (*toast*).

A toast to Newton and a long-lived "Principia." (1999, October 11). *The New York Times,* Section F, p. 4.

Dictionary or Encyclopedia

29. Dictionary (no author listed)

When no author's name is listed on the title page of a dictionary or an encyclopedia, the work is referenced by the title of the work and alphabetized by the first significant word in the title.

Random House dictionary of the English language. (1966). New York: Random House.

30. Encyclopedia (more than one volume, two publishers in two locations)

After the name of the general editor of the encyclopedia, "Ed." is inserted in parentheses, followed by a period. The number of volumes appears in parentheses following the title and then a period. In this case, the title page of the encyclopedia lists two publishers in two locations.

Kazdin, A. E. (Ed.). (2000). *Encyclopedia of psychology* (Vols. 1–8). Washington, DC: American Psychological Association. New York: Oxford University Press.

Doctoral Dissertation or Master's Thesis

31. Doctoral dissertation abstract

The *DAI* (*Dissertation Abstracts International*) volume and page number of the abstract are indicated, ending with a period.

Esposito, J. (1987). Subjective factors and rumor transmission: A field investigation of the influence of anxiety, importance, and belief on rumormongering (Doctoral dissertation, Temple University, 1986). *Dissertation Abstracts International, 48,* 596B.

32. Unpublished doctoral dissertation

If a manuscript copy of the dissertation was used and the *DAI* number is not known, or if an abstract was not published in *DAI,* put the title of the dissertation in italics, write "Unpublished doctoral dissertation," and give the university and location.

Mettetal, G. W. (1982). *The conversation of female friends at three ages: The importance of fantasy, gossip, and self-disclosure.* Unpublished doctoral dissertation, University of Illinois, Urbana.

33. Master's thesis (outside the United States)

If a manuscript copy of a master's thesis was used and the *MAI* (*Master's Abstracts International*) number is not known, or if an abstract was not published in *MAI*, state "Unpublished master's thesis" and the college or university and location. In this case, observe that the title contains a British spelling (*organisational*), which a spell check program might try to "correct."

Hunt, E. (2000). *Correlates of uncertainty during organisational change.* Unpublished master's thesis, University of Queensland, St. Lucia, Queensland, Australia.

Unpublished Material

34. Technical report

The title of a technical report is italicized, followed by the report number in parentheses and the location and name of the organization that issued the report.

LoSciuto, L. A., Aiken, L. S., & Ausetts, M. A. (1979). *Professional and paraprofessional drug abuse counselors: Three reports* (DHEW Publication No. 79-858). Rockville, MD: National Institute on Drug Abuse.

35. Unpublished manuscript

The title of an unpublished manuscript is indicated in italics, followed by "Unpublished manuscript" and the institution and its location.

Burnham, J. R. (1966). *Experimenter bias and lesion labeling.* Unpublished manuscript, Purdue University, West Lafayette, IN.

36. Manuscript submitted for publication (but not yet accepted)

If a manuscript submitted to a publication has not been formally accepted by the editor, then the name of the journal or book publisher to whom the manuscript was submitted should not be displayed. No matter whether the submitted manuscript is for a book, a chapter, or a journal article, the title of the manuscript is italicized.

Mithalal, C. (2005). *Protocols of telephone therapy.* Manuscript submitted for publication.

37. Paper (unpublished) presented at a meeting

The month of the meeting is listed, the title of the paper is italicized, and the name of the sponsoring organization and location of the meeting are indicated.

Rajala, A. K., DeNicolis, J. L., Brecher, E. G., & Hantula, D. A. (1995, May). *Investing in occupational safety: A utility analysis perspective.* Paper presented at the annual meeting of the Eastern Academy of Management, Ithaca, NY.

38. Poster presented at a meeting

The form is the same as the one above.

Freeman, M. A. (1995, August). *Demographic correlates of individualism and collectivism: A study of social values in Sri Lanka.* Poster presented at the annual meeting of the American Psychological Society, New York.

Audiovisual Media

39. Motion picture

After each primary contributor, the particular contribution is noted in parentheses, and "Motion picture" is inserted in brackets after the italicized title of the film. The country of origin (where the film was primarily made or released) and the motion picture studio are indicated.

Zinneman, F. (Director), & Foreman, C. (Screenwriter). (1952). *High noon* [Motion picture]. United States: Universal Artists.

40. Television broadcast

The key here is simply to provide sufficient information to identify the broadcast as best you can, without leaving out any significant identifying detail.

Doyle, W. (Producer). (2001, November 3). *An American insurrection* [Television broadcast]. New York: C-Span 2.

41. Music recording

The information in this example includes the artist's name, the date of copyright, the title of the piece, the recording artist, the title of the album *(Mahler–Bernstein)*, the medium of recording (CD, record, cassette, etc.), and the location.

Mahler, G. (1991). Symphonie No. 8. [Recorded by L. Bernstein & Wiener Philharmoniker]. On *Mahler–Bernstein* [CD]. Hamburg, Germany: Deutsche Grammophon.

Electronic Sources

Some of the more common types of electronic references are illustrated below. However, because new developments in the electronic media are in a constant state of flux, the APA regularly updates its electronic referencing Web site. If you have a specific reference that is not covered by the examples below, or a citation in text of electronic material that was not covered, go to the following APA Web site: http://www.apastyle.org/elecref.html

42. *Abstract retrieved from PsycINFO*

The article is cited in the usual way, but the fact that only the abstract (not the full text) was retrieved is indicated, followed by the date it was retrieved and the Web source.

> Morgeson, F. P., Seligman, M. E., Sternberg, R. J., Taylor, S. E., & Manning, C. M. (1999). Lessons learned from a life in psychological science: Implications for young scientists. *American Psychologist, 54,* 106–116. Abstract retrieved October 14, 1999, from PsycINFO database.

43. *Full-text article retrieved from PsycARTICLES*

The form is the same as the one above, except for the omission of "Abstract" in the retrieval information.

> Egeth, H. E. (1993). What do we *not* know about eyewitness identification? *American Psychologist, 48,* 577–580. Retrieved January 14, 2002, from PsycARTICLES.

44. *Same article retrieved electronically (another option)*

Another suitable option when referencing articles retrieved electronically is to add the words "Electronic version" in brackets after the title, followed by a period, and then the full citation of the printed version.

> Egeth, H. E. (1993). What do we *not* know about eyewitness identification? [Electronic version]. *American Psychologist, 48,* 577–580.

45. *Article in Internet-only journal*

Whenever possible, the URL that links to the article is indicated. If the URL stretches to another line, then it should be broken after a slash or before a period, but do not insert a hyphen at the break.

> Lassiter, G. D., Munhall, P. J., Geers, A. L., Handley, I. M., & Weiland, P. E. (2001, November 1). Criminal confessions on videotape: Does camera perspective bias their perceived veracity? *Current Research in Social Psychology, 2,* 15–22. Retrieved November 2, 2001, from www.uiowa.edu/~grpproc/crisp/crisp.7.1.htm

46. *Information retrieved from Web site*

The host or institutional provider of this information is listed, followed by the date of the document or information (in parentheses, followed by a period), and then the title of the document or information, and finally the date retrieved and the URL.

> American Psychological Association. (1999). Scholarships, grants and funding opportunities. Retrieved October 14, 1999, www.apa.org/students/grants.html

Proofing and Correcting

We now come to the final steps before you submit your paper: proofing and correcting. Read the finished paper more than once, preferably aloud (so you can catch errors like *too* for *to*—which bypass spelling checkers and some grammar checkers). Ask yourself the following questions:

- Are there omissions?
- Are there misspellings?
- Are the numbers correct?
- Are the hyphenations correct?
- Do all the references cited in the body of the paper also appear in the references section?

The first time you read your final draft, the appeal of the neat, clean copy may lead you to overlook errors. Put the paper aside for 24 hours, and then read it carefully again. After you have corrected any errors, give the paper a final look, checking to be sure all the pages are there and in order. If you adhered to the guidelines in this manual, you should feel confident that the paper will receive the serious attention that a clear, consistent, and attractive manuscript deserves.

9

Crafting a Poster and a Concise Report

The poster is a visual display used to convey the nature and major findings of your research in the setting of a public forum. It is customary to provide interested visitors with a concise handout describing the research. The exercise of boiling down your research to its most pertinent components, without sacrificing vital details, will teach you the art of selecting critical information.

Posters and Handout Reports

It is becoming increasingly common for students doing empirical research not only to prepare a detailed written report of their findings, but also to present their results in poster form. Some posters may even be presented at conferences. This format has its own set of conventions and requirements, although they are not uniform; they depend on the parameters set forth by the organizers of each specific conference.

If you have an opportunity to attend a poster session, you can assess the visual impact of the presentations. Which posters draw your eye? What is it about some posters that makes them more visually accessible than others? Poster presenters planning to do further research, or planning to write up their results for submission to a journal, find the feedback they obtain invaluable. If people are not drawn to the poster, however, there is no opportunity for feedback or discussion. Therefore, it is important to create a poster that is visually inviting, and in this chapter we provide guidelines to help you.

To supplement the information that is presented visually in the poster, a concise handout is also usually prepared. The report you prepared for class would be inappropriate as a handout. It is too costly to reproduce a lot of copies of a lengthy paper (the APA asks poster presenters to bring along 50 copies of the research report). Moreover, the paper you wrote for a course contains more information than anyone but your instructor will want.

Therefore, we also illustrate how to condense Jane Doe's detailed research report in appendix A into a concise report for distribution.

Guidelines for the Poster

The way a poster session usually works is that you are asked to show up with your material in a large room or auditorium area, where you will see rows of display boards. Assuming you have not been assigned a particular board, it is first-come, first-served so be sure to arrive early. Pushpins and Velcro hooks are usually available for attaching the pages to the display board. In advance of the meeting, some presenters, having arranged and pasted their pages on a cardboard poster, simply attach the whole poster to the display board. To be safe, it is a good idea to bring extra pushpins. You are not allowed to write, paint, or use paste on the display board, and you must have your display set up in the time allotted (10 minutes, for example), and then your display must be removed and the display board left neat and presentable for the next set of presenters.

Exhibit 15 illustrates how guidelines for poster presentations differ from one organization to another. The exhibit provides a comparison of poster elements distributed by the American Psychological Association (APA) and the American Association for the Advancement of Science (AAAS). In virtually every respect, there is some difference. For example, the AAAS's poster board surface is two feet wider than the APA's; the larger the surface, the more the information that can be displayed. The APA guidelines recommend that an abstract of no more than 300 words be posted in the upper-left corner of the board surface, whereas the AAAS guidelines suggest that the sequence of information begin with the major conclusions.

EXHIBIT 15 APA and AAAS poster design suggestions

Poster Element	APA	AAAS
Poster board surface	4' high, 6' wide	4' high, 8' wide
Legibility	At a 3' distance or more	About a 5' distance
Sequence	Abstract (300 words or less) in upper-left corner, followed by ordered material (use numbers, letters, or arrows)	Conclusions, then supporting text, ending with brief summary
Title and author(s)	1" high, at least	2–3" high
Lettering of text	3/8" high, preferably boldface font, or hand-lettered with regular felt-tipped pen	24-point font, but color as well as different sizes and proportions can be used
Section headings	Clearly labeled headings	1/2–1" high subheadings
Tables and figures	Simple, clear, and easily visible	Graphics preferred to tables
Handouts	50 copies, full paper	Abstract (number unspecified)

It is impossible in this chapter to anticipate every special requirement you may encounter, but you can ensure that your poster will be suitable by finding out the requirements before you begin to design it. To help you get started, Exhibit 16 shows a compact template for a poster of only six $8^1/_2 \times 11$-inch pages and space for the title, author(s), and affiliation heading at the top. The material, allowing for some spacing between the pages and the heading, can be fitted onto a surface approximately 2 feet high and a little over 3 feet wide. The poster board surface furnished by the APA and the AAAS (Exhibit 15) allows the presenter more room to accommodate essential information, whereas Exhibit 16 illustrates how the research can be condensed when less space is available.

As you design your poster, remember that you are trying to draw attention to your study. You also want to chat with people who are interested in learning more about it, as well as to ferret out issues and ideas that can help you anticipate problems if you expect to submit the research to a journal or to continue doing research on this topic. One instructor told us that he cautioned students to be prepared for a cramped area with relatively poor lighting, a lot of distracting noise, and other sensory activity.

Here are three tips to keep in mind:

◆ Choose a font size that is big enough for tired, middle-aged viewers with failing eyesight to see from a distance.
◆ Keep the tables and figures simple, because people don't usually want to stand around and study them.
◆ Keeping it simple also means being selective in what you report, although it doesn't mean being evasive or misleading, only straightforward and concise.

Besides reviewing the specifics provided by the organizer of your poster session, consider these further tips on how to format the poster:

◆ Use a typeface that is easy to read, such as Arial or Times New Roman, not a fancy one that has squiggles or loops.
◆ Make sure that you use a font size that is visible at a distance, such as 24 points (one-quarter inch high; as recommended by the AAAS) or even 32 points.
◆ Don't overcomplicate tables or figures, and don't use jargon or exotic terms that are likely to be unfamiliar to your viewers.
◆ Use color for important highlights, but use it sparingly because you are reporting a scientific study, not creating a work of art.
◆ Make your figures and illustrations bold and self-explanatory, and be sure the details are easy to see.
◆ Organize and label the sequence of information in a way that leads the viewer through the poster, and leave some space to separate the parts of the poster.

Exhibit 17 shows sample text material for a poster using the six-page template in Exhibit 16 and Jane's research results. All that is missing are

EXHIBIT 16   Template for a six-page poster

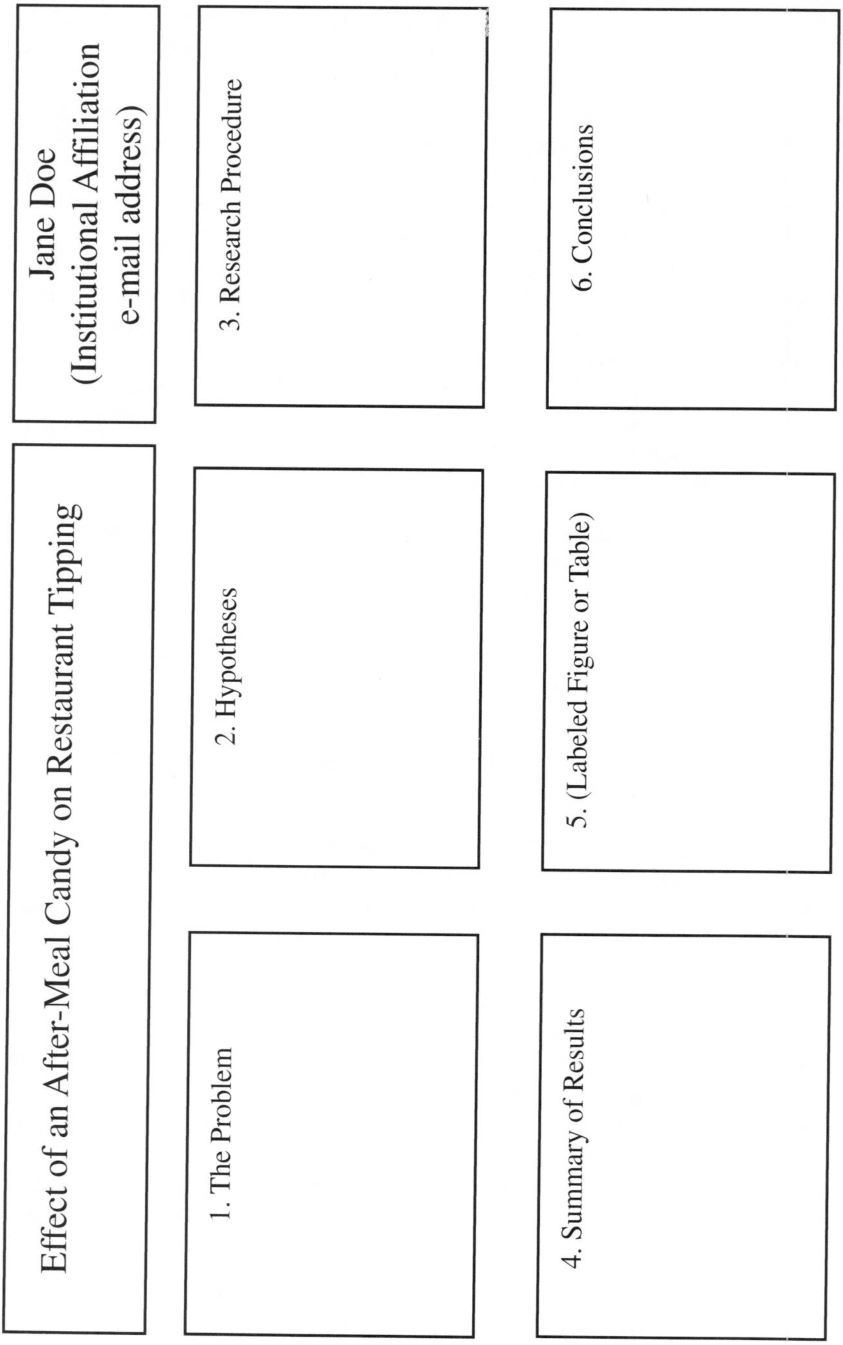

Effect of an After-Meal Candy on Restaurant Tipping

Jane Doe
(Institutional Affiliation
e-mail address)

1. The Problem

2. Hypotheses

3. Research Procedure

4. Summary of Results

5. (Labeled Figure or Table)

6. Conclusions

EXHIBIT 17 *Sample poster content*

1. The Problem

Over 1 million people in the U.S. work as waiters and waitresses who serve in restaurants. Their major source of income is usually the tips they receive from customers. Research on tipping behavior has found that the following techniques used by servers can increase tipping:

- Touching the recipient of the check on the palm of the hand for a fraction of a second.
- Giving diners who are sitting alone a large, open-mouth smile.
- Squatting to the eye level of the dining party.
- Telling the diners one's first name during the initial visit to the table.
- Drawing a happy face or writing "thank you" on the check.

All these techniques seem to have in common that the servers are also doing something that may increase customers' impressions of friendliness. In this study, another such technique was experimentally manipulated— offering the customers an after-meal miniature chocolate candy.

2. Hypotheses

There were three experimental hypotheses:

1. On the assumption that the offer of a miniature chocolate candy would be perceived by diners as a gesture of friendliness, it was hypothesized that the candy offer would encourage tipping behavior, in comparison with a no-candy control condition.

2. On the further assumption that this effect is cumulative (up to a point), it was hypothesized that offering each diner two chocolate candies would encourage tipping even more.

3. Research on reciprocity has found that individuals often feel obliged to return a favor to the person perceived as responsible for the favor. Thus, it was hypothesized that diners' perception that the offer of a second candy reflected the server's spontaneous generosity would encourage tipping still further.

EXHIBIT 17   Continued

---

3. Research Procedure

A waitress in an upscale restaurant in central New Jersey was provided with a small basket filled with wrapped miniature chocolates. She was also given a stack of 80 index cards, each of which indicated one of the following four conditions:

Control condition: The server brought the check (not the basket of candies) at the end of the meal, thanked the dining party, and left the table.

1-piece condition: The server brought the basket of candies when presenting the check, invited each person to select one candy, then thanked the dining party and left the table.

2-piece condition: The server brought the basket of candies when presenting the check, invited each person to select two candies, then thanked the dining party and left the table.

1+1 condition: The server brought the basket of candies when presenting the check, invited each person to select one candy, said, "Oh, have another piece"—as if this were a generous afterthought—and then thanked the dining party and left the table.

---

4. Summary of Results

The dependent measure was the tip percentage, which was obtained for each dining party by division of the amount of the tip by the amount of the check before taxes, and then multiplication by 100. The height of the bars in Figure 1 indicates the mean tip percentage in each condition, and the thin error bars denote the 95% confidence intervals around those mean tip percentages.

As the bar graph shows, the mean tip percentage increased from the control to the 1-piece to the 2-piece to the 1+1 condition. Consistent with this observed trend, a linear contrast was highly significant ($p < .0001$), and the 95% confidence interval for the effect size ranged from $r = .45$ to .73.

Independent-sample t tests of simple effects were also highly significant ($p < .0001$ one-tailed) for the comparison between (a) the control group and the 2-piece condition and (b) the control group and the 1+1 condition (both effect size $rs > .5$). However, the t test comparing the control group and the 1-piece condition was not statistically significant ($p = .17$ one-tailed, effect size $r = .15$), but power was less than .5.

EXHIBIT 17   Continued

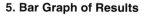

5. Bar Graph of Results

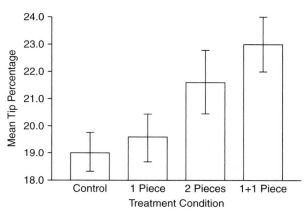

Figure 1. Mean tip percentages and their 95% confidence intervals (based on 20 dining parties in each condition).

6. Conclusions

Offering diners an after-meal chocolate candy increased the tip percentages, and offering two candies increased tips more than offering one. This finding is consistent with the idea that a token gift conveys friendliness, and that, in return, people give larger tips as a sign of their appreciation.

Results in the 1+1 condition were consistent with reciprocity theory, in that people gave the largest tip percentages after being led to believe they had benefited from the server's generous impulse.

Further research is needed to explore the generalizability of these results, as well as research to confirm the mediational roles of friendliness and generosity that were presumed to be operating in this study.

the title of Jane's poster, her name, and her institutional affiliation, all of which would be in boldface, mounted at the top of her poster. You can see that Jane's poster captures the highlights of her research study. If the sponsor requires that you begin with an abstract (as suggested by the APA), try to make it succinct, and let the rest of the poster lead viewers to the results and conclusions. Once you have created your poster, stand back a few feet and see if you can read it easily. You will also want to show it to your instructor, and to any others willing to give candid opinions about its readability and design.

Guidelines for the Concise Report

Because even the most interested viewers are unlikely to want to take extensive notes, have a written report they can take with them. The most economical approach is to try to confine the vital information to two pages, so you can make copies of a one-page handout with information on both sides of the paper. Exhibit 18 illustrates such a handout based on Jane's research. A comparison with her full report in appendix A demonstrates her elimination of superfluous details and her inclusion of only the most essential information. Notice the space provided for Jane's e-mail and institutional mailing address, should anyone wish to communicate with her about this research. Although the poster does not contain a list of references, the handout does.

In preparing your brief report, you will want to consider the same criteria and guidelines that you consulted in developing the major sections of your full report. Your primary obligation is to give people a clear, precise understanding of how the research was done, what you found, and what you concluded. Here are three helpful guidelines:

- Try to anticipate people's questions. For example, think about the comments your instructor wrote on your paper.
- Tell people enough.
- At the very least, report (a) group means, (b) sample sizes, and (c) measurement error, because these minimal raw ingredients are needed for any reanalysis of the results.

Finally, take with you a manila envelope, labeled "HANDOUTS." Slip 50 or more copies of your report inside, and attach it to the poster board, making your research readily available to any interested poster viewers.

EXHIBIT 18   *Concise report for distribution*

Effect of Offering After-Meal Candy on Restaurant Tipping

Jane Doe*
(Institutional affiliation and contact information)

*This brief report is based on a poster of the same title, which was presented at
(name of meeting, date of presentation, location of meeting).*

Background and Hypotheses

More than 1 million people in the U.S. work as waiters and waitresses, and their major source of income is usually from tips (Lynn & Mynier, 1993; Schmidt, 1985). Empirical research has demonstrated that a variety of techniques used by servers can increase tipping, such as (a) briefly touching a diner twice on the palm of the hand (Hornik, 1992); (b) giving a diner who is sitting alone a large, open-mouth smile (Tidd & Lockard, 1978); (c) squatting to the eye level of diners (Lynn & Mynier, 1993); (d) introducing oneself by one's first name at the initial visit to the table (Garrity & Degelman, 1990); and (e) writing "thank you" or drawing a happy face on the check (Rind & Bordia, 1995, 1996).

These techniques seem to have in common that the servers are doing something that may increase customers' impressions of friendliness. This study examined another such technique in a naturalistic experiment, guided by the following three hypotheses:
1. Proceeding on the assumption that offering diners a miniature after-meal chocolate candy would be perceived as a gesture of friendliness, this condition (called the *1-piece condition*) was hypothesized to increase tipping, in comparison with a no-candy *control condition.*
2. Assuming this effect is cumulative, it was hypothesized that offering two pieces of candy (called the *2-piece condition*) would further increase tipping.
3. As people often feel obligated to reciprocate when they have received a favor (Regan, 1971), it was hypothesized that creating the impression that the favor of a second candy was a generous afterthought would increase tipping even more (called the *1+1 condition*).

Method

A waitress in an upscale restaurant in central New Jersey was provided with a basket of wrapped miniature chocolates, which (in all but the control condition) she brought to the table when presenting the check. She was also given a preshuffled stack of 80 index cards, each indicating the particular condition, and the waitress then drew a card blindly from her apron pocket when it was time to present the check. In the *control condition,* she presented the check, thanked the dining party, and immediately left the table. In the *1-piece condition,* she offered each person 1 candy of his or her choice, then thanked everyone and left. In the *2-piece condition,* she offered each person 2 candies of his or her choice, then thanked everyone and left. In the *1+1 condition,* she offered each person 1 candy and said, "Oh, have another piece" (thus making it appear that the favor was a generous afterthought); she then thanked everyone and left. Once the dining party had left the restaurant, the waitress recorded (on the card used to determine the treatment condition) the amount of the tip, the amount of the bill before taxes, and the party size.

*I thank Dr. Bruce Rind for valuable guidance throughout this project, and I thank the owner of the restaurant and the server for making it possible to conduct this study.

EXHIBIT 18 *Continued*

Results

The dependent variable was the tip percentage (i.e., the amount of the tip divided by the amount of the bill before taxes, and then multiplied by 100). The table below summarizes the results in each treatment condition; it shows the mean (M) tip percentage, the 95% confidence interval around M, the standard deviation (SD), and the number (n) of dining parties in each condition:

	Treatment conditions			
Results	Control	1 piece	2 pieces	1+1 piece
M	18.95	19.59	21.62	22.99
95% CI	±0.70	±0.82	±1.17	±1.02
SD	1.46	1.71	2.45	2.43
Sample size (n)	20	20	20	20

These data were analyzed by t tests that compared tip percentages in the experimental and the control condition, using the pooled error term and the corresponding degrees of freedom ($df = 76$). These t tests were statistically significant for the comparison of (a) the 2-piece versus the control condition and (b) the 1+1 piece versus the control condition (p values < .0001, effect size rs of .54 and .70, respectively), but not for (c) the 1-piece versus the control condition ($p = .17$ one-tailed, effect size $r = .15$). A more powerful test was also possible because it was predicted that the tip percentage would increase from the control to the 1-piece to the 2-piece to the 1+1 condition. Addressing this prediction by a linear contrast (λ weights of $-3, -1, +1, +3$ for those 4 conditions, respectively) resulted in $F(1,76) = 44.97$, $p = 3.1^{-9}$, and the effect size $r = .61$ (the 95% CI ranged from $r = .45$ to .73).

Conclusions

The observed pattern of tip percentages (and the linear contrast) was consistent with the prediction that the offer of a token gift of miniature chocolate candy would increase tipping, that offering two candies would increase it further, and that a "generous impulse" offer of a second candy would increase tipping the most. Nonetheless, further research is needed to explore the generalizability of these results, and additional study is also needed to confirm the presumed roles of "friendliness" and "generosity."

References

Garrity, K., & Degelman, D. (1990). Effect of server introduction on restaurant tipping. *Journal of Applied Social Psychology, 20,* 168–172.

Hornik, J. (1992). Tactile stimulation and consumer response. *Journal of Consumer Research, 19,* 449–458.

Lynn, M., & Mynier, K. (1993). Effect of server posture on restaurant tipping. *Journal of Applied Social Psychology, 23,* 678–685.

McCall, M., & Belmont, H. J. (1995). *Credit card insignia and tipping: Evidence for an associative link.* Unpublished manuscript, Ithaca College.

Regan, D. T. (1971). Effects of a favor and liking on compliance. *Journal of Experimental Social Psychology, 7,* 627–639.

Rind, B., & Bordia, P. (1995). Effect of server's "thank you" and personalization on restaurant tipping. *Journal of Applied Social Psychology, 25,* 745–751.

Rind, B., & Bordia, P. (1996). Effect on restaurant tipping of male and female servers drawing a happy, smiling face on the backs of customers' checks. *Journal of Applied Social Psychology, 26,* 218–225.

Schmidt, D. G. (1985). Tips: The mainstay of hotel workers' pay. *Monthly Labor Review, 108,* 50–61.

Tidd, K., & Lockard, J. (1978). Monetary significance of the affiliative smile: A case for reciprocal altruism. *Bulletin of the Psychometric Society, 11,* 344–346.

A

Jane Doe's Research Report

Pages are numbered consecutively, beginning with the title page, and contain a short heading of two or three words from the title.

Restaurant Tipping 1

The student's name and contact address are centered, two double-spaced lines below the title.

Effect of Offering After-Meal Candy on Restaurant Tipping

Jane Doe

(e-mail address or other contact information)

The title is double-spaced if on two lines, in uppercase and lowercase letters and centered between the left and right margins.

Use 12-pt Times Roman or 12-pt Courier typeface, and leave at least 1 inch at the top, bottom, left, and right of each page.

Psy 333: Research Methods

Instructor: Dr. Rind

(date the report is submitted)

The abstract begins on a new page.

Abstract

The abstract is not indented.

Previous research findings were consistent with the idea that restaurant servers can increase their tips by simple techniques that create an impression of the server's friendliness. The experiment reported here was inspired by this idea. The general procedure was having the server personally offer the diners an after-meal candy (i.e., a miniature chocolate) to impress them with her friendliness. In the *control condition,* the server presented the check but brought no candies to the table. In the *1-piece condition,* the server offered each member of the dining party one chocolate candy of his or her choice, and the prediction was that the tip percentage would be greater in this condition than in the control. In the *2-piece condition,* the server offered each diner two candies, on the assumption of a cumulative effect, and the prediction was a further increase in the tip percentage. In the *1 + 1 condition,* the server offered each diner one candy and then said, "Oh, have another piece"; this condition was intended to emphasize the server's generosity and friendliness and was predicted to result in the largest tip percentage. Though tip percentages in the control group differed significantly only from the 2-piece and 1 + 1 conditions, there was, as predicted, an observed increase in tipping going from the control to the 1-piece to the 2-piece to the 1 + 1 condition. A contrast that addressed this observed linear trend was statistically significant, the effect size was $r = .61$, and the 95% confidence interval ranged from $r_{effect\ size} = .45$ to .73. Limitations to the study and suggestions for further research are discussed.

For conciseness, digits are used for all numbers in the abstract, except those that begin a sentence.

Briefly, the abstract tells why the research was done, what was hypothesized, what the results were, and what else appears in the discussion section.

The first line of every paragraph in the text is indented five to seven spaces.

The opening paragraph sets the stage in an inviting way and explains the importance of the research.

The statistical symbol for a percentage (%) is used only when it is preceded by a number.

The text begins on a new page and opens with a repetition of the title.

An ampersand (&) appears in parentheses where "and" is used otherwise.

Although the left margin is even, the right margin is ragged.

Citations buttress the introduction.

Restaurant Tipping 3

Effect of Offering After-Meal Candy on Restaurant Tipping

More than 1 million people in the United States work as waiters and waitresses who serve in restaurants (U.S. Department of Commerce, 1990, p. 391). Although they are generally paid for their service by their employers, their major source of income is usually the tips from customers (Lynn & Mynier, 1993; Schmidt, 1985). Because tips are so important to the livelihood of most servers, knowledge about conditions that affect customers' tipping practices is valuable. Several prior studies have examined factors hypothesized to affect tipping behavior. This research has shown that restaurant servers can increase their tipping percentages by a variety of simple techniques (Lynn, 1996).

Some of these techniques involve direct interpersonal action on the part of the server, such as smiling at or touching the diner. For example, Hornik (1992) had three waitresses at two restaurants either not touch the diners, touch them for half a second on the shoulder, or touch them twice on the palm of the hand for half a second each time. The tips increased from 12% to 14% to 17% in those three conditions, respectively. Tidd and Lockard (1978) had a waitress give a large, open-mouthed smile or a small closed-mouthed smile to diners sitting alone. In the first condition, diners tipped on average more than twice as much as in the second condition. Lynn and Mynier (1993) instructed servers either to squat to the eye level of their customers or stand erect during the initial visit to the table; the squatting resulted in increased tips. Garrity and De gelman (1990) reported that a server earned higher tips when introducing herself by her first name during her initial visit (23% average tip) than when she did not introduce herself (15% average tip).

Other effective techniques used an indirect stimulus to encourage tipping. Rind and Bordia (1996) had two servers either draw or not draw a happy face on the backs of customers' checks before presenting them. The happy face resulted in increased tips for the female server but not for the male server, for whom the customers may have stereotypically dismissed this practice as gender-inappropriate. Rind and Bordia (1995) also found that writing "thank you" on the backs of checks resulted in an increase in tips from 16% to 18%. Finally, McCall and Belmont (1995) had servers present checks either on a tray with credit card emblems on it or on a tray with no emblems and found that tipping percentages were higher in the first condition.

These techniques, except for the last one, have in common that the servers behaved in ways that appeared friendly. The experiment described here explored another technique to create the impression of server friendliness. When presenting the check to the dining party, the server sometimes also offered a treat of assorted miniature chocolates. Three hypotheses were investigated. First, on the assumption that the treat would be perceived by diners as a gesture of friendliness, I predicted that the presentation of the treat would elicit higher tipping than in a no-candy control condition. Second, on the further assumption that this effect is cumulative (up to a point), I predicted that offering more than one candy would stimulate tipping even more. Third, I predicted that creating the impression that a candy treat was a special favor reflecting the server's impulsive generosity and friendliness would increase the tipping still further. This third prediction was consistent with research on reciprocity, which reported that individuals often feel especially obligated to return a favor to the person perceived to be responsible for the favor (Regan, 1971).

Method

Participants

The participants consisted of 80 evening dining parties at an upscale Italian-American restaurant located in central New Jersey, with $n = 20$ dining parties in each treatment condition. The total number of diners was 293, with a mean of 3.67 per dining party ($SD = 1.97$); the size of the dining parties ranged from 2 to 12. A waitress, who served as an experimental accomplice, implemented the four conditions described below.

Materials

The server was provided with a small wicker basket filled with assorted wrapped miniature chocolates. The chocolates were of four types: (a) dark chocolate,

---

Double quotation marks are because "thank you" is the verbatim expression that was used.

Note the orderly presentation of ideas, which tells the instructor that the student has a clear understanding of the project.

First-level headings are centered. Second-level headings are flush left and in italics.

The introduction concludes with your hypotheses or predictions.

All the major sections of the text follow each other without a page break.

The list is lettered for clarity.

Restaurant Tipping 5

(b) milk chocolate, (c) rice-and-chocolate, and (d) peanut butter-and-chocolate. A stack of index cards, which had been thoroughly shuffled beforehand, was placed in the server's apron pocket. Each card described one of the four conditions of the experiment.

Design and Procedure

When it was time to present the check, the server reached into her apron pocket and blindly selected an index card. In the control condition, the card instructed the server simply to present the check in the usual way (not to bring the basket of candy) and then to thank the dining party and to leave the table immediately to avoid any nonessential interaction. In the remaining three conditions, the server was to take along the basket of candy when presenting the check. In the 1-piece condition, the server was to offer each person in the dining party one miniature chocolate of his or her choice, then to thank the diners after their selection of candies and leave the table. In the 2-piece condition, the server was to offer each person in the dining party two miniature chocolates, then to thank the diners after their selection and leave the table. In the 1 + 1 condition, the server was to offer one chocolate and then say, "Oh, have another piece," implying that the favor of a second piece reflected the server's generous afterthought; the server then thanked the diners and left the table. After each dining party left the restaurant, the server recorded (on the same card used to determine the treatment condition) the amount of the tip, the amount of the check before taxes, and the party size.

Results

Scoring and Calculations

Once all information had been collected, I calculated the tip percentage by dividing the amount of the tip by the amount of the check before taxes; I then multiplied the result by 100 to yield a percentage. The raw data and a description of all the analyses can be found in the appendix (following the list of references). I used a computer program to perform the overall calculations, but some analyses were performed on a scientific calculator. The reason for doing some analyses by hand was that the procedures

---

Double quotation there because this was the verbatim statement by the server.

The student mentions that the data and a description of the analyses are in the appendix following the list of references.

The results section follows the method section without a break.

Restaurant Tipping 6

were unavailable on the computer program I used, the formulas were straightforward, and the calculations were relatively simple.

Overall Findings

Basic data. Table 1 (which appears on the next to last page of this report) shows the average tip percentages in the four conditions, that is, the means (M) of the columns of values shown in the appendix. As predicted, the mean tip percentage increased from the control (no candy) to the 1-piece condition, to the 2-piece condition, and to the 1 + 1 condition. Also shown in the table are plus-and-minus 95% confidence estimates for each mean, the standard deviations, and the number of dining parties in each condition. Subtracting from, and adding to, a condition means that the particular confidence estimate shown in this table would yield the lower and upper limits in the population. So, for example, for the control group, there is a 95% probability that the estimated population mean would fall between $18.95 - 0.70 = 18.25$ (the lower limit of the estimated population mean) and $18.95 + 0.70 = 19.65$ (the upper limit of the estimated population mean).

Omnibus F test. Although an overall analysis of variance (ANOVA) did not address my previously stated predictions, I performed such an analysis for two reasons. One was that it was another way to obtain the mean square error (MSE) and thereby served as a check on my other calculations (in the appendix of this report). The other reason was that, given the overall ANOVA used to compute the omnibus F, I could create a summary table showing how the sum of squares (SS) of a contrast F test can be carved out of the overall between-groups SS (shown in Table 2). The omnibus F (numerator $df = 3$, denominator $df = 76$) was 15.51, $p = 5.8^{-8}$, the same result that I would have obtained had the four groups been in any other order.

Focused Statistical Tests[1]

I evaluated the predictions associated with the three hypotheses in this study by three focused statistical tests, with the following results:

Hypothesis 1. The first prediction was that tipping behavior would be greater in the 1-piece than in the control condition. Table 1 shows the direction of the group means to be consistent with this prediction, but an independent-sample *t* test comparing the two groups was not statistically significant even with a one-tailed *p*, where $t(76) = .95$ and one-tailed $p = .17$. The justification for a one-tailed *p* was that I predicted the direction of the effect to be in one tail of the *t* distribution. The corresponding effect size *r*, obtained from the *t* statistic, was .15, and the 95% confidence interval (CI) ranged from $r_{\text{effect size}} = -.17$ to .44, leaving open the possibility of a small effect in the opposite direction from that predicted in the interval containing the population effect size.

Hypothesis 2. On the assumption that the effect of the server's gift giving on subsequent tipping is cumulative, the second prediction was that the tipping would be still greater in the 2-piece than in the control condition. The means in Table 1 are again consistent with the hypothesis, and in this case, the difference between the control condition and the 2-piece condition was statistically significant with $t(76) = 3.99$, $p = 7.5^{-5}$ one-tailed. The effect size *r* associated with this result was .54, and the 95% CI ranged from $r_{\text{effect size}} = .28$ to .73. In other words, there is a 95% probability that this range of values contains the population value of the effect size *r* reflecting membership in the control group versus the 2-piece group as a predictor of the tip percentage.

Hypothesis 3. The third prediction, which I derived from reciprocity theory, was that creating the impression that the server was spontaneously generous (the 1 + 1 condition) would produce the greatest increment in tipping. The *t* test comparing the 1 + 1 condition with the control group yielded $t(76) = 6.05$, $p = 2.5^{-8}$ one-tailed, which has an associated effect size *r* of .70 and a 95% CI ranging from $r_{\text{effect size}} = .50$ to .83.

Contrast F test. To provide a focused evaluation of the increase in tipping from control to the 1-piece to the 2-piece to the 1 + 1 condition, I computed a linear contrast. In a contrast analysis, the prediction of interest is represented by fixed coefficients

---

Degrees of freedom are 76 for this t test, and the p value is denoted as one-tailed.

Each hypothesis is reiterated.

The student uses scientific notation for the p value, where the "–8" tells us to count 8 places to the left of the decimal in 2.5 and make that the decimal place.

95% confidence interval of effect size.

The results are interpreted regarding each hypothesis.

Symbol for "r" is in italics, but the subscript term ("effect size") is not.

A technical term ("lambda weights") is defined.

(lambda weights) that must sum to zero. In this case, the coefficients that represent the linear prediction were $-3, -1, +1, +3$ for the increase from the control to the 1-piece to the 2-piece to the 1+1 groups. The results are summarized in Table 2, which shows the linear contrast carved out of the overall between-groups SS. As indicated, the linear contrast F, with 1 and 76 degrees of freedom, was 44.97, with $p = 3.1^{-9}$ and $r_{\text{effect size}} = .61$; the 95% CI ranged from $r_{\text{effect size}} = .45$ to .73.

For this test, numerator $df = 1$, and denominator $df = 76$.

Discussion

The discussion begins with a statement of the prediction and the results.

I hypothesized that the server's offering an after-meal candy to restaurant diners at the same time she presented the check would have the effect of encouraging tipping, and that the more the candy that was offered, the greater would be the resulting tip percentage. The largest tip percentage was predicted for the condition in which the server was intended to be perceived as spontaneously generous. Though the four group means in Table 1 were consistent with the hypotheses, and the linear contrast F was consistent with the hypothesized linear increase in tipping, the independent-sample t test comparing the control and 1-piece conditions was not statistically significant. However, the power of the t test used to detect the magnitude of effect between the control group and 1-piece conditions was much lower than the recommended level of .80.

The discussion follows the results section without a page break.

The APA manual emphasizes the importance of statistical power in null hypothesis significance testing, particularly when nonsignificant results are reported.

The student discusses the limited statistical power and how it might be improved in future research.

There are many ways to improve statistical power, which refers to the probability of not making a Type II error. These include administering stronger treatments and increasing sample sizes. One way to strengthen the treatments would have been to increase the difference between the number of candies offered, which would also have allowed a further exploration of the idea of a cumulative effect. Because I had to complete this study relatively quickly to meet the course requirement, I could not do such an exploratory replication at this time. However, had there been more than one set of results (i.e., an original study and its replication), then another way to improve statistical power would have been to estimate the overall p value based on a meta-analytic pooling of homogeneous results.

Abbreviation for *id est* ("that is").

Restaurant Tipping 9

Ideas for further investigation are noted.

Further research is also needed to replicate the relationships in this study, particularly to investigate the reliability of the observed findings and the separate and interacting roles of reciprocity and perceptions of friendliness. There is also no evidence that the degree of perceived friendliness was a mediating variable, and this lack of evidence calls for direct empirical evaluation in future research, possibly asking some diners actually to rate the server's friendliness after the bill has been paid and they are about to leave the restaurant. To assess the generalizability of the findings, it is also important in future research to use more than just one server, and to use male as well as female servers, other types of restaurants, and other types of gifts besides chocolates. There may also be regional differences in tipping, which will need to be considered as well.[2]

Superscript number 2 indicates footnote 2, which is shown on the footnotes page in the manuscript.

The references begin on a new page.

References

Garrity, K., & Degelman, D. (1990). Effect of server introduction on restaurant tipping. *Journal of Applied Social Psychology, 20,* 168–172.

Hornik, J. (1992). Tactile stimulation and consumer response. *Journal of Consumer Research, 19,* 449–458.

Lynn, M. (1996). Seven ways to increase servers' tips. *Cornell Hotel and Restaurant Administration Quarterly, 37*(3), 24–29.

Lynn, M., & Mynier, K. (1993). Effect of server posture on restaurant tipping. *Journal of Applied Social Psychology, 23,* 678–685.

McCall, M., & Belmont, H. J. (1995). *Credit card insignia and tipping: Evidence for an associative link.* Unpublished manuscript, Ithaca College.

Regan, D. T. (1971). Effects of a favor and liking on compliance. *Journal of Experimental Social Psychology, 7,* 627–639.

Rind, B., & Bordia, P. (1995). Effect of server's "thank you" and personalization on restaurant tipping. *Journal of Applied Social Psychology, 25,* 745–751.

Rind, B., & Bordia, P. (1996). Effect on restaurant tipping of male and female servers drawing a happy, smiling face on the backs of customers' checks. *Journal of Applied Social Psychology, 26,* 218–225.

Rosnow, R. L., & Rosenthal, R. (2008). *Beginning behavioral research: A conceptual Primer* (6th ed.). Upper Saddle River, NJ: Pearson Prentice Hall.

Schmidt, D. G. (1985). Tips: The mainstay of hotel workers' pay. *Monthly Labor Review, 108,* 50–61.

Tidd, K., & Lockard, J. (1978). Monetary significance of the affiliative smile: A case for reciprocal altruism. *Bulletin of the Psychometric Society, 11,* 344–346.

U.S. Department of Commerce. (1990). *Statistical abstracts of the United States.* Washington, DC: Author.

Annotations:

Issue number of journal paginated by issue.

References with the same authors in the same order are arranged by year of publication.

Author is also the publisher

References are double-spaced in a hanging-indent format, with five-to-seven-space indent.

Journal titles and volume numbers are in italics.

Unpublished manuscript.

Sixth edition.

Capitalize the first word of the title and the subitle.

Capitalize proper nouns in the title.

The appendix begins on a new page.

Appendix

The scores shown below are the tip percentages for each dining party, calculated by division of the tip amount by the check amount before taxes, and then multiplication by 100:

	No candy	1 piece	2 pieces	1 + 1 piece
	18.92	18.87	22.78	17.38
	18.43	20.49	15.81	23.38
	18.67	17.54	19.16	25.05
	18.27	19.35	19.01	21.83
	18.92	20.65	21.60	24.43
	17.84	19.17	18.45	21.11
	19.57	19.73	23.41	25.09
	19.12	17.88	21.37	24.35
	18.67	21.00	22.01	25.37
	22.94	22.33	20.65	21.87
	19.26	19.75	20.92	23.87
	19.49	20.79	26.17	22.62
	19.12	20.52	23.31	26.73
	15.90	22.66	23.85	21.81
	19.29	18.60	22.30	23.60
	19.12	18.60	21.34	23.06
	21.70	20.07	18.89	24.05
	16.72	14.64	23.47	16.72
	17.75	19.01	25.69	22.43
	19.35	20.08	22.12	25.08
M	18.9525	19.5865	21.6155	22.9915
S	1.4948	1.7525	2.5092	2.4898
σ	1.4570	1.7081	2.4457	2.4268

It is not necessary to type the appendix, but it is important to provide the instructor with the raw data that you collected and to provide sufficient details to explain how you computed the results.

Restaurant Tipping 12

All the formulas and the discussion in this appendix are based on the instructor's lectures and the course text. Table 1 lists the 95% confidence intervals (CI) for the four group means, where I computed each CI as follows:

$$M \pm \frac{(t_{(.05)})(S)}{\sqrt{n}}$$

and $t_{(.05)} = 2.093$ for $n - 1 = 19$. For the control group, for example, where $S = 1.4948$, the 95% CI would be

$$\pm \frac{(2.093)(1.4948)}{\sqrt{20}} = \pm 0.6996$$

Thus, adding and subtracting 0.6996 to and from $M = 18.9525$ reveals that there is a 95% probability that the estimated population mean falls between the upper estimate dlimit of 19.6521 and the lower estimated limit of 18.2529.

The pooled error term (MSE) is the average of the squared S values, so $S^2_{pooled} = 4.4502$. The sum of squares between groups ($SS_{between}$) is the total of the squared weighted deviations (weighted by sample size, n_k) between the four condition means (M_k) and the grand mean of $M_G = 20.7865$:

$$SS_{between} = \sum [n_k(M_k - M_G)]$$
$$= 20(18.9525 - 20.7865)^2 + 20(19.5865 - 20.7865)^2$$
$$+ 20(21.6155 + 20.7865)^2 + 20(21.9915 - 20.7865)^2$$
$$= 207.0564$$

In the summary ANOVA in Table 2, the omnibus F test (with numerator $df = 3$ and denominator $df = 76$) is defined as follows:

$$F = \frac{SS_{between}/(k-1)}{S^2_{pooled}} = \frac{207.0564/3}{4.4502} = 15.5091$$

Formulas can be written in by hand, if that is easier.

The calculations are reported in a way that walks the reader through the logical sequence used, clearly explaining how the summary results in the research report were obtained.

Independent-sample t tests, using the pooled error term above and $df = N - k$ (corresponding to this mean square error term), compared the 1-piece versus control, the 2-piece versus control, and the $1+1$ piece versus control by the following formulas:

$$t = \frac{M_1 - M_2}{\sqrt{\left(\frac{1}{n_1} + \frac{1}{n_2}\right) S_{pooled}^2}}, \quad \text{and } r_{\text{effect size}} = \sqrt{\frac{t^2}{t^2 + df}}$$

where df for the effect size $r = n_1 + n_2 - 2$. Substituting in these formulas the data for the 1-piece versus control comparison, the analyses were

$$t = \frac{19.5865 - 18.9525}{\sqrt{\left(\frac{1}{20} + \frac{1}{20}\right) 4.4502}} = 0.9504, \quad \text{and } r_{\text{effect size}} = \sqrt{\frac{(.9504)^2}{(.9504)^2 + 38}} = .1524$$

Contrast weights for the hypothesized linear increase in tipping from control to 1-piece to 2-piece to $1+1$ condition were $-3, -1, +1, +3$. Correlating these weights with the four group means yielded $r_{\text{alerting}} = .9831$, and squaring this value indicated the proportion of SS_{between} that accounted for the linear contrast. Multiplying the squared alerting r (.9665) by SS_{between} (207.0564) resulted in the contrast sum of squares shown in Table 2. I calculated the effect size r for the contrast as follows:

$$r_{\text{effect size}} = \sqrt{\frac{F_{\text{contrast}}}{F_{\text{contrast}} + F_{\text{noncontrast}}(df_{\text{noncontrast}}) + df_{\text{within}}}} = \sqrt{\frac{44.9688}{44.9688 + 0.7793(2) + 76}} = .6058$$

The results, although rounded to two decimal places in the text, are not rounded in the calculations.

The student explains the calculations, indicating her depth of understanding to the instructor.

The author note begins on a new page.

Author Note

I thank the owner of the restaurant for giving me permission to conduct this research, and I thank the server who kindly participated in the experiment (both requested anonymity). The results of this study will be shared with them, as they requested. I also thank Dr. Bruce Rind for his guidance throughout this project.

The author note in a student's paper is the place to acknowledge the assistance of others.

The author note is not usually a requirement in a student's paper.

The footnotes begin on a new page.

Footnotes

[1]The term *focused tests* means that the statistical tests are precisely oriented to the prediction, that is, as opposed to omnibus tests, which are diffuse and unfocused. Examples of focused tests are all F tests with numerator $df = 1$ and all t tests, whereas an example of omnibus tests is all F tests with numerator $df > 1$. Whenever there is a specific prediction regarding the direction of the results that involves more than two groups or conditions, focused tests can be used to address that prediction, and these focused tests are usually more powerful than omnibus tests and lend themselves to interpretable effect size indices (Rosnow & Rosenthal, 2008, p. 317).

[2]On a personal note, I plan to try out the after-meal 1 + 1 candy strategy when I return to my summer job as a waitress in Ogunquit, Maine, after this semester.

It is not necessary always to have footnotes in a student's paper. But if you use them, this is the APA style.

Table 1 begins on
a new page.

Table number
and title (which
is in italics) are
flush left.

Table 1

Mean Tip Percentage (M), 95% Confidence Interval (CI) of Mean, Standard
Deviation (SD), and Number of Sampled Dining Parties (n)

Row and
column
headings are
telegraphic.

When means
are reported, an
associated
measure of
variability is
also reported.

Results	Treatment conditions			
	Control	1 piece	2 pieces	1 + 1 piece
M	18.95	19.59	21.62	22.99
95% CI	±0.70	±0.82	±1.17	±1.02
SD	1.46	1.71	2.45	2.43
Sample size (*n*)	20	20	20	20

Note. The mean (*M*) value denotes the average tip percentage in the particular
condition. The 95% CI is the confidence interval around the obtained estimate of
the population mean. Tip percentages were calculated for each dining party by
division of the tip amount by the bill amount before taxes, then multiplication by
100. The standard deviation (*SD*) is the variability of *n* = 20 tip percentages around
the sample mean.

Table notes are
placed below
the table, and
in this case, the
note clearly
explains what
appears in the
table.

Tables are placed
after the references,
author note, and
footnotes, each
table on its own
separate page.

Table 2 begins on
a new page.

Table 2

Analysis of Variance with Linear Contrast

Because the linear and noncontrast sums of squares were carved out of the between-groups sum of squares, the carved-out sources are slightly indented to represent this fact.

Source	SS	df	MS	F	$r_{effect\ size}$
Between groups	207.06	3	69.02	15.51*	–
Linear contrast	200.12	1	200.12	44.97*	.61
Noncontrast	6.94	2	3.47	0.78	–
Within error	338.22	76	(4.45)		

The mean square error (MSE) is enclosd in parentheses.

Note. The value enclosed in parentheses under MS is the mean square error (MSE). No effect sizes are reported in this table for the two omnibus F tests (i.e., numerator $df > 1$) as "the rule of thumb is to report effect sizes for focused statistical procedures and not for omnibus statistical procedures, because effect size indicators are far more interpretable for focused procedures" (Rosnow & Rosenthal, 2008, p. 321).

The page number of the quoted material is indicated.

*$p < .0001$.

The APA style is to use asterisks or daggers to identify probability levels in tables.

The APA style is to round values to two decimal places in tables to make the tabular values read more easily in tables that contain a lot of information.

B

John Smith's
Review Paper

Pages are numbered consecutively, beginning with the title page, and contain a short heading of two or three words from the title.

Concept of Intelligence 1

The Elusive Concept of Intelligence:

Two Diverse Theoretical Orientations

The title is double-spaced if on two lines, in uppercase and lowercase letters and centered between the left and right margins.

The student's name and contact address are centered, two double-spaced lines below the title.

John Smith

(e-mail address or other contact information)

Use 12-pt Times Roman or 12-pt Courier typeface, and leave at least 1 inch at the top, bottom, left, and right of each page.

Psy 222: Psychological Testing

Instructor: Dr. Skleder

(date the term paper is submitted)

The abstract begins on a new page.

The abstract is not indented.

The term *g* is italicized.

Abstract

Although the study of intelligence has a long history in psychological and educational research, the concept of intelligence remains one of the most elusive. Going back to the psychometric work of Charles Spearman, many psychological and educational researchers have regarded intelligence as *g*-centered, which means that they assume a general trait (*g*) lies at the core of every valid measure of intelligence. More recently, leading researchers, such as Howard Gardner, Robert J. Sternberg, and Stephen J. Ceci, have theorized the existence of distinct facets of intelligence that are not all *g*-centered. The purpose of this review is to examine these two diverse theoretical orientations, with the focus on Gardner's theory of multiple intelligences as a prominent example of the more recent orientation. I discuss criticisms and rejoinders with respect to the theoretical notion of multiple intelligences, and the paper concludes with a brief summation and overview of the principal theme of this review.

The abstract tells why the paper was written and, very briefly, what the paper argues or explains in the context of its purpose.

The first line of every paragraph in the text is indented five to seven spaces.

Page number of the quoted passage.

Book titles are italicized.

Concept of Intelligence 3

The text begins on a new page and opens by repeating the title.

The Elusive Concept of Intelligence:

Two Diverse Theoretical Orientations

In 1971, in an article in *The Encyclopedia of Education,* Harry B. Gilbert observed that "no clear agreement exists among psychologists and educators with respect to the nature of intelligence" (p. 128). Judging from more recent discussions of this topic in popular textbooks on psychological testing, it seems there is still no universal agreement about the nature, or even the definition, of intelligence. Indeed, Kaplan and Saccuzzo (2005) stated that "of all the major concepts in the field of testing, intelligence is among the most elusive" (p. 231). In another popular textbook in this area, Anastasi and Urbina (1997) wrote that "the unqualified term 'intelligence' is used with a wide diversity of meanings, not only by the general public but also by members of different disciplines, such as biology, philosophy, or education . . ., and by psychologists who specialize in different areas or identify with different theoretical orientations" (p. 294).

In everyday parlance, for example, some individuals are called *book smart,* ostensibly a synonym for traditional academic intelligence. Some people are referred to as *street smart,* a term implying that they are intellectually shrewd in the ways of the world. Some are said to have *business savvy* or *political sense* or *the ability to read people like a book,* phrases meaning that the person's intellectual abilities involve certain interpersonal aptitudes that are not directly assessed by standard tests of academic IQ.[1] The purpose of this review is to explore the elusive and controversial nature of the concept of intelligence from the perspective of both the traditional and a more recent theoretical orientation. Both are associated with a substantial, and still growing, body of research and speculation, and both have proponents and detractors in the intelligence research community. Indeed, enough has been said and written about the concept of intelligence to fill an encyclopedia (*Encyclopedia of Human Intelligence,* 1994).

Stephen J. Ceci (1996), a proponent of the more recent view of intelligence as multifaceted, argued that the traditional theoretical orientation can be reduced to

Defined terms are italicized.

Superscript number 1 indicates footnote 1, which is shown on the footnotes page later in the manuscript.

Concept of Intelligence 4

"five easy facts . . . that are known to all members of the intelligence research community" (p. 4). These facts include (a) that virtually all people tend to score relatively consistently on different tests of intelligence; (b) that, using a statistical procedure called factor analysis, there emerges a first principal component (called *g*) that reflects the average correlation among test scores, and it is generally around .30; (c) that *g* is a proxy for general intelligence; (d) that there have been impressive correlations reported between *g* and academic and social accomplishment; and (e) that intelligence is heritable to a considerable degree. Having listed those "five easy facts," Ceci then mounted an attack on the theoretical implications of each, arguing that a plausible alternative model exists for each fact. "Intelligence is a multifaceted set of abilities," Ceci (1996) contended, and any "specific facet might become more or less effective as a result of the physical, social, cultural, and historical contexts in which it has been crystallized and the contexts in which it is subsequently assessed" (p. 8).

Two Issues in Intelligence Assessment

Before a specific discussion of the two major divergent views, it is important to note that the assessment of intelligence is also problematic to some degree. One problem that Gilbert (1971) mentioned was that, "since human beings are complex, observing or measuring intelligence is no simple matter" (p. 129); he gave the following illustration:

> Observe star quarterback Joe, for example. It is Friday afternoon, last period, social studies. The teacher, Mr. Jones, is expounding his pet topic, "The Obsolete Electoral College: Or Is It?," while Joe's mind is on tomorrow's game. When Mr. Jones asks, "Joe, what do you think?" Joe is about to say, "Pass to the right end," but he returns to reality and mumbles something about not being sure of the answer. (p. 129)

Someone who did not know Joe very well might quickly conclude from his mumbled response that he is not especially bright or motivated. Joe is, in fact, strongly motivated and intelligent, although his motivation and intellect are consumed by his

The list is lettered for clarity.

All the major sections of the text follow each other without a page break.

First-level heading is centered.

A quotation of 40 or more words is set off from the body of the text by means of indented margins.

Although the left margin is even, the right margin is ragged.

Concept of Intelligence 5

anticipation of the next day's football game and his role as quarterback, not by the electoral college. Joe is running complex plays through his mind; hence, "Pass to the right end" is almost his reply to the teacher's question. From an empirical perspective, the point here is that intelligence is indeed an elusive concept.[2] ——————————————————— Footnote 2.

    Another issue involves the generalizability of population norms, such as the tables of values that are available for standard tests of intelligence and are used to decide where a person's performance falls relative to the performance of the general population. Suppose a psychological or educational researcher with a limited budget has developed a new test of academic IQ. To establish the population norms, the researcher issues a call for volunteers to take the new test, for example, students who will receive a small compensation or who will satisfy a course requirement. But evidence has accumulated on the relationship between volunteering for research and scores on standard IQ tests, and it suggests that, "when there is a significant relationship reported, and very often

Abbreviation for id est ("that is").

there is, it is overwhelmingly likely to show volunteers to be more intelligent" (i.e., they score higher) than the general population (Rosenthal & Rosnow, 1975, p. 68).

    The threat to generalizability of the researcher's estimated population norms from using volunteer subjects is a specific case of sampling bias, as illustrated in Figure 1 (at the end of this paper). The figure shows, in an approximate way, the positive bias predicted to result from using a volunteer sample instead of doing random sampling from a national probability data set. The distribution that is labeled X represents a theoretical normal distribution of the IQs of volunteers for the researcher's IQ test, whereas Y represents a theoretical distribution of the IQs of people in general. The extent to which the mean of X is different from the mean of Y implies bias that jeopardizes the generalizability of the volunteer-standardized population norms. In other cases, the use of volunteers can lead to underestimates of vital population parameters, but in this case the implication of Figure 1 is that standardizing the new test only on volunteers will probably yield overestimates of normative scores in the general population.

The student mentions Figure 1.

Concept of Intelligence 6

The Traditional Theoretical Orientation

Early Contributors

Second-level heading is flush left and in italics.

The intelligence-testing movement began with the measures adopted by researchers such as Francis Galton in England and James Cattell in the United States, who theorized that sensory input and reaction time, inasmuch as they are critical in the acquisition and processing of information, are also fundamentally important indicators of intellectual differences (Benjamin, 2004; Gilbert, 1971). However, following Galton's inspiration for the correlation coefficient and its mathematical refinement by the great statistician Karl Pearson, it was shown that the early measures used in the intelligence-testing movement were unrelated to school performance. As a consequence, those "anthropomorphic tests" (a term used by Benjamin, 2004, p. 12) were replaced by the paper-and-pencil scales developed in Paris by Alfred Binet and Henri Simon "to help diagnose the existence of mental retardation as distinguished from mental illness and resulting dementia" (Gilbert, 1971, p. 130). Gilbert noted that although "intelligence testing originated in Europe in at least two separate movements . . . the greatest development of intelligence tests bears a distinct 'made in U.S.A.'" (p. 130). The earliest adaptation of Binet's testing method for the American marketplace was by Henry Goddard, but the Stanford-Binet adaptation and its use by Lewis Terman in 1916 (and revised in 1937) are better known. In 1939, David Wechsler, at the Bellevue Hospital in New York, developed an individual intelligence test for adults, which was revised in 1955 and called the Wechsler Adult Intelligence Scale, or WAIS (Kaplan & Saccuzzo, 2005).

The g-Centered View

Influenced by the psychometric work of Charles Spearman (1927), who viewed intelligence as a general factor (*g*), psychological and educational researchers in the intelligence test movement pretty much accepted as valid the *g*-centric idea. A number of prominent intelligence researchers, such as Arthur Jensen (1969), argued that differences in *g* could be attributed largely to heritability (genetic factors) as opposed to environmental

Citations in parentheses are in the same order in which they appear in the reference list.

A quoted passage within the quoted passage in the text is set off by single quotation marks.

An ampersand (&) appears in parentheses where "and" is used otherwise.

or cultural influences (cf. Vandenberg, 1971). Child development researchers, inspired by the theoretical and empirical work of Jean Piaget, also argued for the idea of general structures of the mind, structures that developed in a similar way in all children (Siegler & Richards, 1982). In the biological area, some investigators have attempted to operationalize *g* by measuring the speed of neural transmission (Reed & Jensen, 1992), or by measures of hemispheric localization (Levy, 1974). In the 1990s, a controversial reanalysis of IQ test data by Herrnstein and Murray (1994), in a book entitled *The Bell Curve,* ignited a spirited debate about the presumed role of *g* in the lives of individuals and in the larger social order. The traditional *g*-centric view has been periodically challenged, but it is also apparently true that, as Ceci (1996) argued, a great many psychological and educational researchers consider fundamental the idea that standard tests of intelligence provide numbers that allow us to distinguish "bright" people from the "not-so-bright" in terms of accrued knowledge or the potential for learning.

In sum, whether psychological and educational researchers mean by *intelligence* (a) the ability to adapt to the environment, (b) the ability to deal with symbols or abstractions, or (c) the ability to learn, it is also true that many researchers have assumed that a core ingredient in such aptitudes is the factor known as *g* (Gilbert, 1971). Recently, Frey and Detterman (2004) argued that the Scholastic Assessment Test (SAT) is basically a surrogate measure of general intelligence (*g*) and can be used to predict cognitive functioning. In one study, these researchers extracted a measure of *g* from the Armed Services Vocational Aptitude Battery and found the correlation with SAT scores to be *r* = .82 (or .86 corrected for nonlinearity) in a sample of 917 subjects aged 14–21 from a national probability data set. In a second study, they used a sample of 104 undergraduate students, recruited through the psychology subject pool, to investigate the relationship between SAT scores and scores on another test, called Raven's Progressive Matrices (a test of reasoning skills), and found *r* = .483 (or .72 corrected for restricted range).

Abbreviation for confer ("compare") is used in parentheses.

Book title is italicized.

This abbreviation is first spelled out for the reader.

Concept of Intelligence 8

The Multiplex Theoretical Orientation

An early criticism of the traditional view of intelligence was expressed by L. L. Thurstone (1938) and his coworkers. On the basis of psychometric studies that they conducted with large numbers of participants, Thurstone and Thurstone (1941) concluded that there are distinct aptitudes, which they called "primary mental abilities," including verbal comprehension, word fluency, numerical ability, and spatial relations. More recently, Sternberg and Berg (1986) reported that a panel of experts embraced diverse, and ostensibly divergent, factors in what they theoretically associated with intelligence. Although controversy continues to surround the meaning of intelligence as well as its relationship to real-world skills, a Task Force of the American Psychological Association (APA) was nevertheless able to agree on a list of "knowns" about intelligence (Neisser, Boodoo, Bouchard, Boykin, Brody, Ceci et al., 1966). Yet, as early as 1971, Gilbert's prescient answer to the question of whether intelligence is a "general characteristic" or instead consists of a number of "relatively independent abilities" was that "modern theory tends to support the latter view, although there are dissenters" (p. 129).

Four years earlier, in a book entitled *The Nature of Intelligence,* J. P. Guilford (1967) proposed that ordinary intelligence encompasses multiple aptitudes and raised the possibility of over 100 different ways in which individuals can excel intellectually. A generation later, moving the idea of multiple aptitudes in another direction, Robert Sternberg (1990) argued that the nature of the information-processing measured by standard IQ tests is quite different from that involved in certain kinds of complex reasoning in everyday life. For example, Ceci and Liker (1986) found that skill in handicapping racehorses could not be predicted from scores on the WAIS. Sternberg, Wagner, Williams, and Horvath (1995) stated that "even the most charitable estimates of the relation between intelligence test scores and real-world criteria such as job performance indicate that approximately three-fourths of the variance in real-world performance is not accounted for by intelligence test performance" (p. 912).[3]

The first full citation of a work lists up to six authors.

Abbreviation for et alia ("and other").

Footnote 3.

Concept of Intelligence 9

Sternberg's (1985, 1988, 1990) own triarchic theory and Ceci's (1990, 1996) bioecological theory are representative of a theoretical orientation that might be called *multiplex* because it encompasses several distinct types of intelligence.[4] Another prime example of this orientation is the focus of the remainder of this review, namely, the theory of multiple intelligences proposed by Howard Gardner (1983, 1993b).

Gardner's Idea of Multiple Intelligences

Eight Criteria of Intellectual Talents

Gardner (1983, 1993b) argued against the assumption of a single general characteristic and used the term *intelligences* (plural) to convey the idea of multiple intellectual aptitudes. Gardner's (1983) general definition of intelligence is that it encompasses "the ability to solve problems, or to create products that are valued within one or more cultural settings" (p. x). He went on to argue that not every real-life skill should be considered under the label of *intelligence,* though any talent deemed "intellectual" must fit the following eight criteria:

1. The potential must exist to isolate the intelligence by brain damage.

2. Exceptional populations (such as savants) whose members manifest outstanding but uneven abilities should exhibit the distinctive existence of the particular type of intelligence.

3. There must be identifiable core operations, that is, basic information-processing operations that are unique to the particular abilities.

4. There must be a distinctive developmental history, that is, stages through which individuals pass, with individual differences in the ultimate levels of expertise achieved.

5. There should be locatable antecedents (more primitive, less integrated versions) of the intelligence in other species.

6. The intelligence must be open to experimental study, so that predictions of the construct can be subjected to empirical tests.

Side annotations:

Footnote 4.

The writer emphasizes that Gardner's theory is of multiple intelligences.

Indicates that the reference list shows more than one work by this author that was published in 1993b.

Numbering the eight criteria sets them off for clarity.

Concept of Intelligence 10

7. Although no single standardized test can measure the entirety of the abilities that are deemed intellectual, standardized tests should provide clues about the intelligence and should predict the performance of some tasks and not others.

8. It must be possible to capture the information content in the intelligence through a symbol system, for example, language or choreographed movements.

Seven Types of Intelligence

Using as a base the eight criteria listed, Gardner argued the importance of studying people within the "normal" range of intelligence, and also of studying those who are gifted or expert in various domains valued by different cultures (Gardner, 1993a). He further emphasized the importance of studying people who have suffered selective brain injuries. Drawing on the eight criteria above and the research results from four major disciplines (i.e., psychology, sociology, anthropology, and biology), Gardner (1983) proposed the existence of seven types of intelligence: (a) logical-mathematical, (b) linguistic, (c) spatial, (d) bodily-kinesthetic, (e) musical, (f) intrapersonal, and (g) interpersonal. Subsequently, he raised the possibility of additional types of intelligence (Gardner, 1999), but this review focuses on his original seven types.

Traditional intelligence, which is language-based and easy to quantify by conventional measures, encompasses *logical-mathematical intelligence* and *linguistic intelligence,* Gardner explained. People who score high in logical-mathematical intelligence are good at reasoning and computation. Presumably, this skill is also what Frey and Detterman (2004) extracted from the tests they correlated with the SAT. People with keen linguistic skills are adept with words and language. Gardner also maintained, however, that these two types of intelligence represent only part of the intellectual picture, and he posited five additional types.

Spatial intelligence is exhibited by people who navigate the spatial world with great ease. *Bodily-kinesthetic intelligence* is the domain of dancers, athletes, neurosurgeons, and others skilled in carrying and moving their bodies. A person who is *musically intelligent* is

Another list lettered for clarity.

Concept of Intelligence 11

talented in discerning themes in music and is sensitive to qualities of melody (e.g., pitch, rhythm, and timbre). The last two intelligences are part of what Gardner termed the "personal intelligences," that is, the talent to detect the various shades of meaning in the emotions, intentions, and behavior of oneself (*intrapersonal intelligence*) and others (*interpersonal intelligence*). Those people who score high on intrapersonal intelligence are adept at self-understanding; those who score high on interpersonal intelligence are "people persons" who have a fix on the social and interpersonal landscape.

Independence of Abilities

Crucial to Gardner's formulation is the assumption that the various intellectual "talents" are not necessarily linked. Someone may perform poorly in one area (e.g., logical-mathematical intelligence) and yet perform well in others (e.g., spatial intelligence). This discrepancy calls to mind the stereotype of the brilliant but absent-minded scientist, who cannot find his or her car in the parking lot but can describe in intricate detail the workings of atoms, and perhaps of automobiles. Different intelligences can coexist and can presumably be measured quite independently of one another, according to Gardner's theory. However, he argued, because logical-mathematical and linguistic intelligences are valued so highly in our society, tests designed to measure a variety of intelligences still rely heavily on these particular skills to the exclusion of other intellectual talents (Gardner, 1991b, 1993b).

In other words, Gardner's argument is that conventional tests of intelligence measure essentially the same intelligences in only slightly different, and perhaps trivial, ways. Therefore, it is hardly surprising that Spearman (1927) found a medium-sized correlation among certain abilities (implying the *g* factor), so that individuals who score higher in verbal intelligence tend to score higher than average in reasoning ability. Knowing someone's linguistic intelligence, however, does not automatically tell us very much about the person's skills with people or music, or about the person's intellectual talents in any other realm, according to this argument.

Abbreviation for exempli gratia ("for example") is used in parentheses.

Indicates more than one work in 1991 and more than one work in 1993 by this author in the reference list.

Concept of Intelligence 12

The independence of abilities is also suggested by the fact that, although intelligence tests can predict school grades reasonably well, the tests are far less useful in predicting routine successes outside the school setting. For example, barring low levels of traditional IQ, good managerial skills may be related more to the ability to manage oneself and the task completion of others, or to the ability to interpret the actions and intentions of others, than to the ability to score high on a standard IQ test or some surrogate measure of academic intelligence (Aditya & House, 2002; Sternberg, 1988). Sternberg (1988, p. 211) described these extracurricular skills as "practical intelligence" (and distinguished them from academic IQ); such practical intelligence seems to depend heavily on what Gardner called the "personal intelligences."

Some Criticisms and Rejoinders

Nontraditional Orientation

Some criticisms of multiplex theories of intelligence appear to rest on the distinction between innate ability and performance skills that have been traditionally characterized as *talent* (Walters & Gardner, 1986). Ericsson and Charness (1994) argued that expert performance does not usually reflect innate abilities and capacities but is mediated predominantly by physiological adaptation and complex skills. Gardner's (1995) response was that the issue is not whether children are born with innate abilities or capacities, but whether a child who has begun to work in a domain finds a skill and ease in performance that encourage him or her to persevere in the effort. That most people do not usually think of performance skills as "intellectual" is just a red herring in this debate, a reflection of our continued attachment to the traditional idea of intelligence, Gardner argued. Sternberg (1990) noted that a person who has experienced an injury that causes a loss of bodily-kinesthetic ability is not viewed as "mentally retarded."

In short, Gardner's argument is that all the forms of intelligence he proposed should be given equal consideration with the logical-mathematical and linguistic forms so highly valued in Western cultures (Walters & Gardner, 1986). As he put it, "When one revisits

First-level headings are centered, where as second-level headings are flush left and in italics.

the psychological variable that has been most intensively studied, that of psychometric intelligence or *g*, one finds little evidence to suggest that sheer practice, whether deliberate or not, produces large ultimate differences in performance" (Gardner, 1995, p. 802). Perhaps it is because experts have chosen to regard *g* and the "academic intelligences" as more important than the personal intelligences that terms like *socially retarded* are not common. However, interest in social proclivities appears to be leading to increased attention to the interplay of the personal intelligences and behavior in different situations, such as predicting achievement or success in executive positions in organizations (e.g., Aditya & House, 2002).

Structure and Amenability to Operationalization and Assessment

Another criticism of multiplex theories of intelligence is that, given their seemingly amorphous nature, there would appear to be unlimited possibilities of adding to the number of intelligences. As noted, Gardner himself raised the possibility of more than seven intelligences and considered the original seven "working hypotheses" that are fully amenable to revision after further investigation (Walters & Gardner, 1986). For example, Gardner (1999) alluded to the "naturalist intelligence" of a Charles Darwin and the "existential intelligence" of a postmodern philosopher. With all these additions, one may wonder whether they might eventually be psychometrically reduced to general types, an idea that may suggest the return to a (Spearman-like) general factor (as well as specific factors). However, whether this criticism is perceived as reasonable probably depends on one's willingness to regard the concept of intelligence as even more inclusive of human talents than it is now.

Also, it has been argued that the standard psychometric approach has the distinct advantage of being more amenable to testing and measurement than is Gardner's theory of multiple intelligences. Gardner, on the other hand, contended that his seven intelligences are measurable but that conventional tests are inadequate for the job. He proposed measurements that are closely linked to what people do in their daily lives. For example,

The arguments are developed logically and persuasively.

Concept of Intelligence 14

in applying his theory to education, Gardner (1991a, 1993b) reported assessing children's intelligences by studying their school compositions, choice of activities in athletic events, and other aspects of their behavior and cognitive processes. Although this approach is certainly more complex and time-consuming than the older approach, such measurements are essential from the standpoint of Gardner's theory.[5]

Footnote 5.

Conclusions

Over three decades ago, Gilbert (1971) cautioned that "the use of intelligence tests too often has preceded understanding of the nature of intelligence and the limitations of tests" (p. 135). This review has concentrated on Gardner's theory as an illustration of recent work on human intelligence. Gardner's work encompasses some traditional aspects and, at the same time, attempts to move our conceptualization of intelligence beyond the classic boundaries. For example, when Gardner (1983) described a great dancer as "kinesthetically intelligent," he alluded to a skill that Spearman would not have accepted as belonging within the category of intelligence. That Gardner's theory is much broader than the traditional notion of intelligence is viewed by some as problematic because the broader the theory, the more difficult it is to disprove. Nonetheless, there appears to be a trend toward broad, interdisciplinary formulations and definitions or, as Sternberg (1997) conceptualized them, whatever mental abilities are necessary to enable persons to shape and adapt to their environment.

All sections continue without a page break.

Within such a broader theoretical orientation, researchers have explored ways of assessing and improving performance skills that in the past were ignored or considered far less significant than academic intelligence (e.g., Aditya & House, 2002; Gardner, 1991b; Gardner, Kornhaber, & Wake, 1996; Sternberg, Torff, & Grigorenko, 1998). Another direction of recent work on intelligence was discussed by Anastasi and Urbina (1997), who mentioned that, in the field of developmental psychology, researchers have found "substantial correlations between ratings of infant behavior on personality variables and subsequent cognitive development" and also that "studies of the environmental-mastery

The conclusions wrap up the discussion, reviewing the objective of the paper first.

The student gives his own impressions of trends and future directions.

Multiple citations in parentheses are in the order shown in the list of references.

motive in infants have revealed some promising relations to subsequent measures of intellectual competence" (p. 302). The challenge still remains not only to improve our understanding of the elusive concept of intelligence but also, as Wesman (1968) put it, to do "intelligent testing" (p. 267). It is important to develop innovative approaches, no matter how complex and nontraditional, to measure the different facets of intellectual capabilities (Gardner et al., 1996; Neisser et al., 1996; Sternberg, 1992) and, more fundamentally, to recognize that intelligence is "a result of one's total life experience" (Gilbert, 1971, p. 135).

While raising some issues, the final paragraph clearly ends the discussion.

The references begin on a new page.

References

Aditya, R. N., & House, R. J. (2002). Interpersonal acumen and leadership across cultures: Pointers from the GLOBE study. In R. E. Riggio, S. E. Murphy, & F. J. Pirozzolo (Eds.), *Multiple intelligences and leadership* (pp. 215–240). Mahwah, NJ: Erlbaum.

Anastasi, A., & Urbina, S. (1997). *Psychological testing* (7th ed.). Upper Saddle River, NJ: Prentice Hall.

Benjamin, L. T., Jr. (2004). Meet me at the fair: A centennial retrospective of psychology at the 1904 St. Louis World's Fair. *APS Observer, 17*(7), 9–12.

Ceci, S. J. (1990). *On intelligence . . . more or less: A bioecological treatise on intellectual development.* Englewood Cliffs, NJ: Prentice Hall.

Ceci, S. J. (1996). *On intelligence: A bioecological treatise on intellectual development* (Expanded ed.). Cambridge, MA: Harvard University Press.

Ceci, S. J., & Liker, J. (1986). Academic and nonacademic intelligence: An experimental separation. In R. J. Sternberg & R. Wagner (Eds.), *Practical intelligence: Nature and origins of competence in the everyday world* (pp. 119–142). New York: Cambridge University Press.

Encyclopedia of human intelligence. (1994). New York: Macmillan.

Ericsson, K. A., & Charness, N. (1994). Expert performance: Its structure and acquisition. *American Psychologist, 49,* 725–747.

Frey, M. C., & Detterman, D. K. (2004). Scholastic assessment or *g*? The relationship between the Scholastic Assessment Test and general cognitive ability. *Psychometric Science, 15,* 373–378.

Gardner, H. (1983). *Frames of mind: The theory of multiple intelligences.* New York: Basic Books.

Gardner, H. (1991a). Assessment in context: The alternative to standardized testing. In B. R. Gifford & M. C. O'Connor (Eds.), *Changing assessments: Alternative views of aptitude, achievement and instruction* (pp. 77–119). Boston: Kluwer.

Page numbers of this chapter.

Capitalize the first word of the title and the subtitle of an article or a book.

Editors.

Major cities can be listed without a state abbreviation.

Concept of Intelligence 17

Gardner, H. (1991b). *The unschooled mind: How children think and how schools should teach.* New York: Basic Books.

Gardner, H. (1993a). *Creating minds: An anatomy of creativity seen through the lives of Freud, Einstein, Picasso, Stravinsky, Eliot, Graham, and Ghandi.* New York: Basic Books.

Gardner, H. (1993b). *Multiple intelligences: The theory in practice.* New York: Basic Books.

Gardner, H. (1995). Why would anyone become an expert? *American Psychologist, 50,* 802–803.

Gardner, H. (1999). *Intelligence reframed: Multiple intelligences for the 21st century.* New York: Basic Books.

Gardner, H., Kornhaber, M. L., & Wake, W. K. (1996). *Intelligence: Multiple perspectives.* Ft. Worth, TX: Harcourt Brace.

Gilbert, H. B. (1971). Intelligence tests. In L. C. Deighton (Ed.), *The encyclopedia of education* (Vol. 5, pp. 128–135). New York: Macmillan & Free Press.

Guilford, J. P. (1967). *The nature of intelligence.* New York: McGraw-Hill.

Herrnstein, R. J., & Murray, C. (1994). *The bell curve: Intelligence and class structure in American life.* New York: Free Press.

Jensen, A. R. (1969). How much can we boost IQ and scholastic achievement? *Harvard Educational Review, 39,* 1–123.

Kaplan, R. M., & Saccuzzo, D. P. (2005). *Psychological testing: Principles, applications, and issues* (6th ed.). Belmont, CA: Thomson Wadsworth.

Levy, J. (1974). Cerebral asymmetries as manifested in split-brain man. In M. Kinsbourne & W. L. Smith (Eds.), *Hemispheric disconnection and cerebral function* (pp. 165–183). Springfield, IL: Thomas.

Neisser, U., Boodoo, G., Bouchard, T. J., Jr., Boykin, A. W., Brody, N., Ceci, S. J., Halpern, D. F., Loehlin, J. C., Perloff, R., & Urbina, S. (1996). Intelligence: Knowns and unknowns. *American Psychologist, 51,* 77–101.

Proper names in title are capitalized.

"Ed." for one editor.

Volume and page numbers.

Sixth edition of book.

The APA style is to list up to six authors, but (for clarity) this student lists all the authors.

Concept of Intelligence 18

Random House dictionary of the English language (Unabridged ed.). (1996). New York: Random House.

Reed, T. E., & Jensen, A. R. (1992). Conduction velocity in a brain nerve pathway of normal adult correlates with intelligence. *Intelligence, 16,* 259–272.

Rosenthal, R. (1990). How are we doing in soft psychology? *American Psychologist, 45,* 775–777.

Rosenthal, R., & Rosnow, R. L. (1975). *The volunteer subject.* New York: Wiley.

Rosenthal, R., & Rosnow, R. L. (2008). *Essentials of behavioral research: Methods and data analysis* (3rd ed.). New York: McGraw-Hill.

Rosnow, R. L., Skleder, A. A., Jaeger, M. E., & Rind, B. (1994). Intelligence and the epistemics of interpersonal acumen: Testing some implications of Gardner's theory. *Intelligence, 19,* 93–116.

Siegler, R. S., & Richards, D. D. (1982). The development of intelligence. In R. J. Sternberg (Ed.), *Handbook of human intelligence* (pp. 897–971). New York: Cambridge University Press.

Spearman, C. (1927). *The abilities of man.* New York: Macmillan.

Sternberg, R. J. (1985). *Beyond IQ: A triarchic theory of human intelligence.* New York: Cambridge University Press.

Sternberg, R. J. (1988). *The triarchic mind: A new theory of human intelligence.* New York: Viking.

Sternberg, R. J. (1990). *Metaphors of mind: A new theory of human intelligence.* New York: Cambridge University Press.

Sternberg, R. J. (1992). Ability tests, measurements, and markets. *Journal of Educational Psychology, 84,* 134–140.

Sternberg, R. J. (1997). The concept of intelligence and its role in lifelong learning and success. *American Psychologist, 52,* 1030–1037.

Unabridged edition.

Third edition of book.

Journal title and volume number are in italics.

Concept of Intelligence 19

Sternberg, R. J., & Berg, C. A. (1986). Definitions of intelligence: A comparison of the 1921 and 1986 symposia. In R. J. Sternberg & D. K. Detterman (Eds.), *What is intelligence? Contemporary viewpoints on its nature and definition* (pp. 155–162). Norwood, NJ: Ablex.

Sternberg, R. J., Torff, B., & Grigorenko, E. L. (1998). Teaching triarchially improves school achievement. *Journal of Educational Psychology, 90,* 374–384.

Sternberg, R. J., Wagner, R. K., Williams, W. M., & Horvath, J. A. (1995). Testing common sense. *American Psychologist, 50,* 912–927.

Thurstone, L. L. (1938). *Primary mental abilities.* Chicago: University of Chicago Press.

Thurstone, L. L., & Thurstone, T. G. (1941). *Factorial studies of intelligence.* Chicago: University of Chicago Press.

Vandenberg, S. G. (1971). Genetics of intelligence. In L. C. Deighton (Ed.), *The encyclopedia of education* (Vol. 5, pp. 117–128). New York: Macmillan & Free Press.

Walters, J. M., & Gardner, H. (1986). The theory of multiple intelligences: Some issues and answers. In R. J. Sternberg & R. K. Wagner (Eds.), *Practical intelligence: Nature and origins of competence in the everyday world* (pp. 163–181). New York: Cambridge University Press.

Wesman, A. G. (1968). Intelligent testing. *American Psychologist, 23,* 267–274.

Authors' names are inverted, but the editors of the book in which this article appears are not inverted names.

Ampersand is used properly, even though it is not in parentheses.

The author note begins on a new page.

Concept of Intelligence 20

Author Note

I thank Professor Robert Rosenthal for permission to reproduce the graphic indicated as Figure 1 in this paper (personal communication, April 10, 2007). The graphic originally appeared as Fig. 4-2 on p. 128 in Rosenthal and Rosnow (1975). I thank Dr. Anne Skleder for her guidance throughout this project and fo rexplaining the problem with the percentage-of-variance interpretation of effect size and directing me to the statistical references cited in footnote 3.

The author note is not usually a requirement in a student's paper.

The footnotes begin on a new page.

Footnotes

[1]The symbol *IQ* originally stood for the intelligence quotient, which, when it was introduced, was defined as the ratio of the person's mental age (as measured by an IQ test) to the person's chronological age. Anastasi and Urbina (1997) also stated, however, "For the general public, IQ is not identified with a particular type of score on a particular test but is often a shorthand designation for intelligence" (p. 295).

[2]As taught in this course, all observations and psychological testing methods are limited in some ways, and it is frequently very helpful to use multiple observations or methods to zero-in on concepts of interest (such as intelligence, in this case).

[3]It can be noted, though, that finding a predictor variable that accounts for approximately one quarter of the variance (i.e., an effect size correlation of around .5) is not unimpressive in psychological research (Rosenthal, 1990). It has also been documented that many important effects in experimental trials in the field of biomedicine are far smaller than $r = .5$ (Rosenthal & Rosnow, 2008, pp. 325–326). However, Sternberg et al.'s (1995) point that conceptual and psychometric limits exist in the traditional model of intelligence is well taken and supportive of the argument that intelligence consists of "various, relatively independent, abilities" (Gilbert, 1971, p. 129).

[4]I chose the word *multiplex* because all these theories of multiple intelligences reminded me of a movie theater in which different films are playing to different audiences in auditoriums that are all clearly separated from one another and yet are housed in the same building. The first definition of *multiplex* in the *Random House Dictionary of the English Language* (1966) is "manifold; multiple" (p. 940).

[5]Dr. Skleder directed me to some research along this line in which she had been involved (Rosnow, Skleder, Jaeger, & Rind, 1994). The research reported a series of successful replication studies testing the implications of Gardner's (1983) proposal of a developmental trajectory in the ability to read other people's motives and intentions, an ability called *interpersonal acumen* by these researchers.

It is not necessary always to have footnotes in a student's paper. But if you use them, this is the APA style.

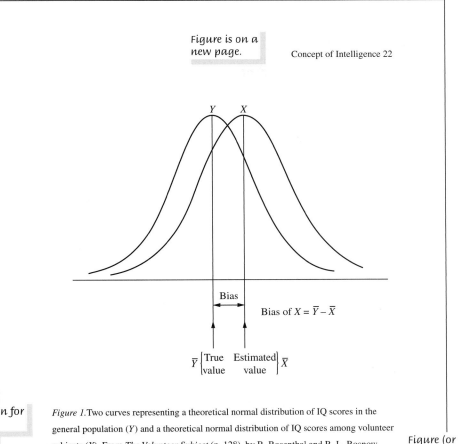

Figure is on a new page.

Concept of Intelligence 22

Caption for figure.

*Figure 1.*Two curves representing a theoretical normal distribution of IQ scores in the general population (*Y*) and a theoretical normal distribution of IQ scores among volunteer subjects (*X*). From *The Volunteer Subject* (p. 128), by R. Rosenthal and R. L. Rosnow, 1975, New York: Wiley. Copyright by authors. Reprinted with permission.

Figure (or table) from another source requires permission to reproduce or adapt.

Index

TO THE OWNER OF THIS BOOK:

I hope that you have found *Writing Papers in Psychology,* Eighth Edition useful. So that this book can be improved in a future edition, would you take the time to complete this sheet and return it? Thank you.

School and address: _____

_____

Department:

Instructor's name: _____

1. What I like most about this book is:_____

_____

_____

2. What I like least about this book is:_____

_____

_____

3. My general reaction to this book is:_____

_____

_____

4. The name of the course in which I used this book is:_____

_____

5. Were all of the chapters of the book assigned for you to read?_____

    If not, which ones weren't?_____

6. In the space below, or on a separate sheet of paper, please write specific suggestions for improving this book and anything else you'd care to share about your experience in using this book.

_____

_____

DO NOT STAPLE · PLEASE SEAL WITH TAPE

FOLD HERE

- -

BUSINESS REPLY MAIL

FIRST-CLASS MAIL   PERMIT NO. 34   BELMONT CA

POSTAGE WILL BE PAID BY ADDRESSEE

Attn: Michele Sordi, Psychology Department

Wadsworth

10 Davis Drive

Belmont, CA 94002-3098

Il.l...l..lll..ll....l.l.l.l..l.l.ll...ll...ll

- -

FOLD HERE

OPTIONAL:

Your name: _____ Date: _____

May we quote you, either in promotion for *Writing Papers in Psychology,*
Eighth Edition, or in future publishing ventures?

Yes: _____ No:_____

Sincerely yours,

Ralph L. Rosnow and Mimi Rosnow